GREEN TRANSPORTATION

RESEARCHED & WRITTEN BY

MS. BEDATRI ANAND

MRS. SHARDA KUMARI

MR. KANHAIYA JEE ANAND

MR. UTAKARS ANAND

TANEESHA PUBLISHERS

Title   :   Green Transportation

Author   :   Bedatri Anand

Edition   :   1st (September, 2023)

ISBN   :   978-81-19580-29-3

Published by

TANEESHA PUBLISHERS | *A Venture of -*
PRACHI DIGITAL PUBLICATION

Regd. Add.: 254, Khuriyakhatta No. 10, Bindukhatta,
Lalkuan, Nainital - 262402, Uttarakhand, India
Website : www.taneeshapublishers.in
E-mail : info@prachidigital.in
Contact : +91-976041-7980, 845481-2712

Printed by :
Techshresta Solutions Pvt. Ltd., Bengaluru - 560025, Karnataka

Dedicated to Beloved

Mrs. Draupdi Devi (Mother), Mrs. Anita
Devi (Bhabhi)
& Late Ramchandra Prasad Singh

Special Dedication to the Team of Engineer
Live Foundation for Support and Help.

INDEX

14. What is the Economics of Green Transportation ?

15. What is CONCLUSION of the GREEN
TRANSPORTATION ?

16. Enclosures

A. Cross section of Street Road, Village
Road, Highway, Expressway

B. Junction of Street Road-Village Road, Village Road-
Village Road, Highway-Highway & Expressway-
Expressway.

PREFACE

BOLBAM TIRTH (TRAVEL TO SHIVALINGAM PUJA) IS A PHYSICAL AND CHEMICAL SCIENCE

Barefoot walking of more than 100 km is a practical class in between the human body to learn Complete Physics, Chemistry, Biology, Engineering, Medicine and Economics.

GREEN TRANSPORTATION which should be friendly of Nature or Road which does not disturb the Quality of Nature such that no disturbances should occur in ETHER, AIR, HEAT, WATER, EARTH, FOOD and ENVIRONMENT.

Green Transportation should have Connectivity to the Airport Junction, Port Junction, Railway Junction and Space Junction.

We Traveled Devghar in Barefoot with Elder Shri Rajniti Prasad Singh, Younger Kamal kishore, Bhai Hira, Bhai Arbind Kumar, & Bhai Rajkumar. In Traveling we discussed and reached a idea to have a book on Green TRANSPORTATION.

Sawan, Bhado Khas month and other months Special.

BOLBAM YATRI IN BABADHAM TEMPLE

BOLBAM YATRI ON GREEN ROAD

CHAPTER-I

Introduction

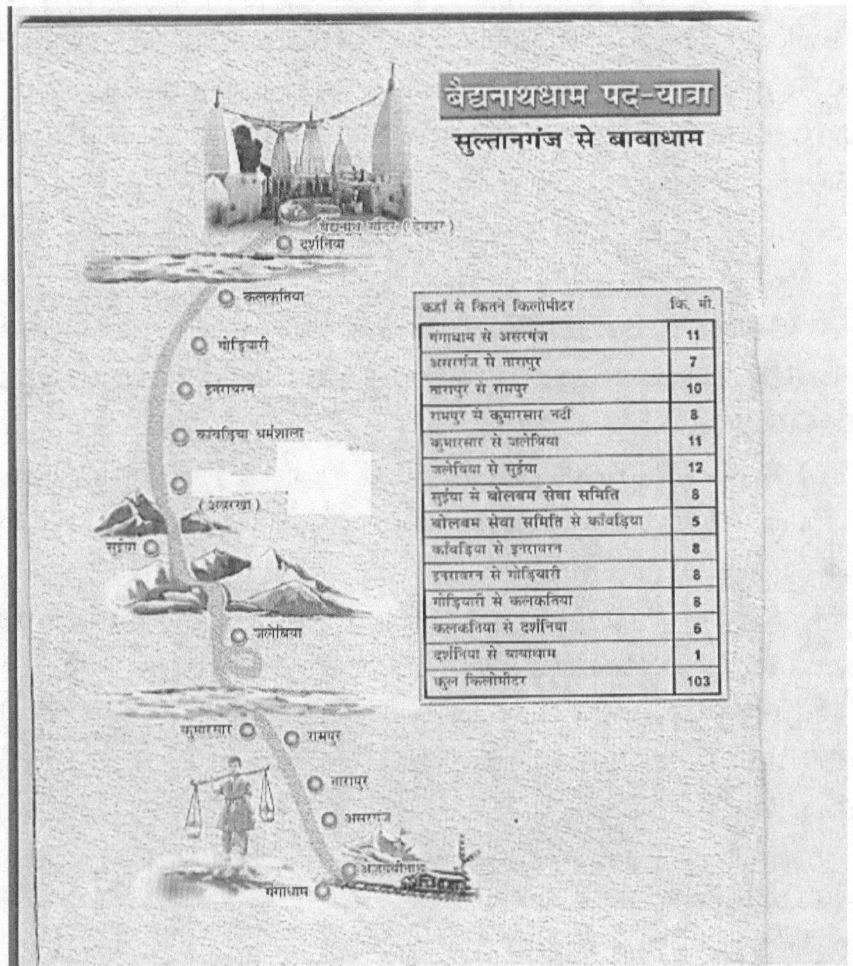

कहाँ से कितने किलोमीटर	कि. मी.
गंगाधाम से असरगंज	11
असरगंज से तारापुर	7
तारापुर से रामपुर	10
रामपुर से कुमारसार नदी	8
कुमारसार से जलेबिया	11
जलेबिया से सुईया	12
सुईया से बोलबम सेवा समिति	8
बोलबम सेवा समिति से कांवड़िया	5
कांवड़िया से इनरावरन	8
इनरावरन से गोड़ियारी	8
गोड़ियारी से कलकतिया	8
कलकतिया से दर्शनिया	6
दर्शनिया से बाबाधाम	1
कुल किलोमीटर	103

Crores of People taking morning dip in Uttarayani ganga and collecting Uttarayani Gangajal with Mantra and fixing targets to put on Babadham and Basuki Dham and great challenges taken by people and people are fulfilling these challenges.

Mainly five auspicious way people are taking challenge to perform this activity is as under.-

1. FASTING BAM-Barefoot Travel to keep water in Kawariya on Shoulder in Fasting (Fruits and Juice is allowed to eat).This is very special and Important Bam.On the way whenever Bam feeling Urine or Pressure to go Latrine, Bam has to keep the Jal on auspicious place, then he can move to urine pass and Latrine and after finishing BAM has to compulsorily take the Bath further BAM has to take up the JAL to perform puja for further movement.

2. NORMAL BAM-Barefoot Travel to keep water in Kawariya on Shoulder without Fasting (Food is allowed).Rest procedure as the FASTING BAM.

3. DAK BAM-Keeping Energized Gangaajal behind the head and traveling 110 km to Baba dham in 20-24 hours without going bath without taking water in Barefoot.

4. SASTANG BAM-By Sastang.It takes Months to reach the Destination.Rest procedure as per FASTING BAM.

5. BICYCLE BAM-Traveling by Bicycle to follow the Rules of FASTING BAM is also common.BAM is running the Bicycle with Barefoot.

Apart from above now, a day following THREE BAM is also considered for travel.

1. MOTORCYCLE BAM-Traveling with Motor Cycle with Barefoot and following the rules of FASTING BAM, but this is not a Common BAM and safety point of view this is illegal.

2. BUS/CAR BAM-Traveling with BUS/CAR with Barefoot and

following the rules of FASTING BAM.

3. TRAIN/FLIGHT BAM-Traveling with TRAIN/FLIGHT with Barefoot or without Barefoot and following the rules of FASTING BAM.

Barefoot walking & Benefit

1. The Empty foot walk or Sastang of 155 km, that too with the blessed Uttarayan Ganga water, is beneficial for health.

2. Supernatural vision.

3. Supernatural Service Culture.

5. Purity of the body.

6. Chanting of the supernatural power mantra, **BOL BOMB**.

7. Unprecedented **SElf DEPENDENT BUSINESS**.

8. Natural bodily Physical and Chemical hygiene action which cures all diseases related to body fat, BP, sugar and five elements (Ether, Air, Fire, Water & Earth) related.

9. Expenses - Walking on empty feet or Sastang with energized Ganga water.

REQUIREMENT OF BIHAR/JHARKHAND/ORISSA STATE

1. The Bitumen dangerous road from Sultanganj to Ganga bank should be made a **GREEN ROAD.**

2. Pedestrian roads should be made by putting one foot from the silt of Ganga, and peepal neem, Bargad & mango plants should be planted on both sides.

3. In the nine kilometers which is near Jharkhand, sand of the river has also been poured, which pricks the feet and the body, in its place one feet of Ganga silt should be put. If the Jharkhand government is not able to do it, then the Bihar government should do it or some other organization should do it.

4. The arrangement of borebels should be increased, especially in Jharkhand and around the Gorayari river.

5. Deoghar to Basukinath road should also be made from the sand of the Ganges. It will be easy to walk to Sastang.

6. Bitumen and concrete roads need to be converted into **Green Roads**, so that crores of devotees can walk or Sastang comfortably.

7. Airports should be constructed at Lakhisarai, Sultanganj and Bhagalpur so that outsiders can carry Uttarayani GangaJal and perform Jalabhishek on foot or Sastang. Deoghar has an airport.

8. All the houses near the temple in Deoghar, Indra-damneshwar Dham, Kageswar Dham, Basukinath Dham, Hariharnath Dham, Garibnath Dham and other Dham in India should be demolished. The place to sell Prasad should be shifted to bus stand, railway station, airport and other places away from Dham area and plant should be planted including Green House of Dham Pujari and Green Ashram(Height of Green building should be lower than the Temple) to stay of BAM in 10000 acres around the temple.

9. To understand practically the difference between Tirth/pilgrimage and tourism, the world has to come Bihar/Jharkhand/Orissa to understand.The following has to create Green Road is as under-

Ajgaibinath Dham (Sultanganj) - Babadham (Deoghar) - Basukinath Barefoot walk, Sanstang pilgrimage-155km

Bhagalpur - Basukinath - Deoghar Barefoot walk, Sastang pilgrimage-155km

Hathidah/Barahiya - Indradamneshwar Dham (Ashokgham) - Kageshwar Gham (Jamui) - Babadham (Deoghar) - Basukinath Dham Barefoot walk, Sanstang pilgrimage-155km

Pahleja Ghat Sonpur - Hariharnath Dham (Sonpur) - Garibnath Gham (Muzaffarpur) - 70 KM

Buxar - Brahmpur Dham - Gupta Dham - 120KM

Singheshwarnath Dham (Maghepura) - Aguani Ghat (Sultanganj) - 60 KM

Someshwar Nath Gham, Areraj' Motihari - Gandak River - 30 km

Cuttack(Mahanadi River and Gadagadia Ghat) to Jagannath Temple and Loknath Temple in Puri - 81 km

Here few question is raised to discuss is as under-

1.   How is Bodily Physical and Chemical Hygiene Action which cures all diseases related to body fat, BP, Sugar and Five Elements (Ether, Air,

Fire, Water & Earth) related (FIVE ELEMENTS & PHYSICAL HEALTH)?

2. What is the difference between pilgrimage(TIRTH) and Tourism?

3. Why is the Bolbam Tirth Extreme in Sawan, Bhado, Average in Asin and Karthik and Lower in other months?

4. Why Uttarayani Ganga Jal?

5. Why Morning Dip in Uttarayani Ganga?

6. Why barefoot Walking on Earth 110 km?

7. Why is the BOLBAM Mantra chanted?

8. How does this activity Purify the Body?

9. How Self Dependent Business is Developing with Innovative Ideas?

10. How will the Bolbam Yatra become much Effective?

11. Why Green Road?

12. What is the Bolbam Tirth & Green Road Concept?

13. What is the Economics of Green Road?

14. What is CONCLUSION OF THE BOLBAM TIRTH & GREEN ROAD CONCEPT?

Now we are in position to discuss How is Bodily Physical and Chemical Hygiene Action which cures all diseases related to body fat, BP, Sugar and Five Elements(Ether, Air, Fire, Water & Earth)related as under-

CHAPTER-2

What is FIVE ELEMENTS & PHYSICAL HEALTH?

Health is always depending on the equilibrium position of Five Elements Ether, Air, Fire, Water & Earth

According to Vedic science, when Spirit (*Purusha* in Sanskrit) takes the form of life it is called *Prakriti*.

Prakriti is made up of five elements from finest to grossest: space, air, fire, water and earth. In Sanskrit they are called *Akash, Vayu, Agni, Jal,* and *Prithvi,* respectively.

Every individual is a microcosm of nature and therefore contains all five elements. Let us examine each.

As Spirit takes form it passes first through space or Akash. The Akash element corresponds to awareness itself. It is the layer beyond the other four gross elements and is responsible for the transmission of sound, including mantra.

It is the home of potential and possibility.

Akash animates Vayu or air, which allows for movement and thought, and it connects us to the sense of touch and the all-important breath.

Akash and Vayu combine to form the Vata dosha in Ayurveda.

Fire comes next and is responsible for heat, desire, motivation and the sense of sight. It allows us to want something, see where we are going as we get it, and digest it once we have it.

Agni allows for transformation and Agni dominates the Pitta dosha.Fire and Water combine is the reason for Pitta Dosha.

Fire then animates water or Jal, permitting flux, emotion, cohesion and the sense of taste. Excess Jal will lead to unnecessary emotional and sensory dependence.

Lastly, physical form corresponds to earth or Prithvi. Anything we can smell contains Prithvi. It is the seat of stability when balanced. The land of Earth interacts with and influences climate heavily since the surface of the land heats up and cools down faster than air or water

Jal and Prithvi together create the Kapha dosha.

The spiritual path is walked in reverse, however, from gross to fine. Prithvi allows the body to become stable, followed by the balancing of Jal, emotion and senses. The stable body and emotions vanquish the struggle of Agni, desire. With deep breathing, Vayu, we connect to the present moment. Finally, experiencing the Akashic realm, one rests in his true nature. The Yogic Masters tell us that God-consciousness is beyond all of it.

Uncontrolled Vata, Pitta and kapha Dosha causing POSITION OF DEATH(MARNASANNA)

Unbalanced Dosha causing problems in Human Body needs help.Human being moved to Allopathy Doctor to cure, while any disturbances in Dosha can be controlled to just walk 110 km continuously in a disciplined manner.

We will understand this technology systematically in the next chapter.

Now we are in position to discuss the important issue difference between pilgrimage(TIRTH) and Tourism.

CHAPTER-3

What is the Difference between Pilgrimage(TIRTH) and Tourism?

TIRTH-

TIRTH is a place where People perform such controlled activity to control the Five Elements Akash, Vayu, Agni, Jal, Prithvi and 3 sensitive elements are control of Man or Sense, Budhi or Intellect and Ahankar or Ego.

Tirtha is "one of the many ways toward self-realization and bliss".

Tirtha can be an actual physical sacred location in Hindu traditions, or a metaphorical term referring to meditation where the person travels to an intellectual sacred mind state such as of "truth, forgiveness, kindness, simplicity and such".

Take an Example of Tirth.Let us take example of KUMBH TIRTH of Prayag.People from various places reaching to Prayag to take DIP in SANGAM.

How people reach SANGAM.

1. Barefoot walking of more than 10km.

2. Taking DIP in Ganga in Group.

3. Taking SUNBATH to gain energy from SUN.

4. Drinking Pure GANGA WATER.

5. Staying in ASHRAM and eating the Satvik food prepared by self or by Ashram.Performing Sewa to required places like cleaning the Way of Ganga, Room, Ghat preparation, Performing Morning and Evening Arti etc.

6. Following the strict technology of BRAHMACHARYA

7. Saint who is continuously involved in Devotion organizing PRAVACHAN.

8. Hotel also behaves like ASHRAM itself, hence Hotel is not required in TIRTH.

9. All above positive Energy Creates a Positive Magnetic Field.

People who devote themselves to taking DIP for a few days in GANGA, really are getting the benefit of Control of FIVE ELEMENT and THREE INTERNAL ELEMENT.

TOURISM-

Tourism is a social, cultural and economic phenomenon which entails the movement of people   to countries or places outside their usual environment for personal or business/professional purposes.

What is the main purpose of tourism?

Tourism **boosts a sense of cultural exchange between foreigners and citizens** for Social, Cultural and Economic Phenomenon.

Tourism products

According to the World Tourism Organization, a tourism product is:

"A combination of tangible and intangible elements, such as natural, cultural, and man-made resources, attractions, facilities, services and activities around a specific center of interest which represents the core of the destination marketing mix and creates an overall visitor experience including emotional aspects for the potential customers. A tourism product is priced and sold through distribution channels and it has a life-cycle".

Tourism product covers a wide variety of services including:

• Accommodation services from low-cost homestays to five-star hotels

- Hospitality services including food and beverage serving centers
- Health care services like massage
- All modes of transport, its booking and rental
- Travel agencies, guided tours and tourist guides
- Cultural services such as religious monuments, museums, and historical places
- Shopping

Various types of tourism

A. Mass tourism

Academics have defined mass tourism as travel by groups on pre-scheduled tours, usually under the organization of tourism professionals.

B. Niche tourism

Niche tourism refers to the numerous specialty forms of tourism that have emerged over the years, each with its own adjective. Many of these terms have come into common use by the tourism industry and academics.Others are emerging concepts that may or may not gain popular usage.Ex-Film Tourism etc.

C. Sustainable tourism

Sustainable Tourism is a concept that covers the complete tourism experience, including concern for economic, social and environmental issues as well as attention to improving tourists' experiences and addressing the needs of host communities.

Sustainable tourism should embrace concerns for environmental protection, social equity, and the quality of life, cultural diversity, and a dynamic, viable economy delivering jobs and prosperity for all.

D. Ecotourism

Ecotourism, also known as ecological tourism, is responsible travel to fragile, pristine, and usually protected areas that strive to be low-impact and (often) small-scale. It helps educate the traveler; provides funds for conservation; directly benefits the economic development and political empowerment of local communities, and fosters respect for different cultures and for human rights.

E. Volunteer tourism

Volunteer tourism (or voluntourism) is growing as a largely Western phenomenon, with volunteers traveling to aid those less fortunate than themselves in order to counter global inequalities.

F. Pro-poor tourism

Pro-poor tourism, which seeks to help the poorest people in developing countries, has been receiving increasing attention by those involved in development; the issue has been addressed through small-scale projects in local communities and through attempts by Ministries of Tourism to attract large numbers of tourists.

G. Recession tourism

Recession tourism is a travel trend which evolved by way of the world economic crisis. Recession tourism is defined by low-cost and high-value experiences taking place at once-popular generic retreats. Various recession tourism hotspots have seen business boom during the recession thanks to comparatively low costs of living and a slow world job market suggesting travelers are elongating trips where their money travels further.

H. Medical tourism

When there is a significant price difference between countries for a given medical procedure, particularly in Southeast Asia, India, Sri Lanka, Eastern Europe, Cuba and Canada] where there are different regulatory regimes, in relation to particular medical procedures (e.g. dentistry), traveling to take advantage of the price or regulatory differences is often referred to as "medical tourism".

I. Educational tourism

Educational tourism is developed because of the growing popularity of teaching and learning of knowledge and the enhancing of technical competency outside of the classroom environment.

J. Event tourism

This type of tourism is focused on tourists coming into a region to either participate in an event or to see an organized event put on by the city/region

K. Creative tourism

Creative tourism has existed as a form of cultural tourism, since the early beginnings of tourism itself. Its European roots date back to the time of the Grand Tour, which saw the sons of aristocratic families traveling for the purpose of mostly interactive, educational experiences.

L. Experiential tourism

It is an approach to traveling which focuses on experiencing a country, city or particular place by connecting to its history, people, food and culture.

M. Dark tourism

This type of tourism involves visits to "dark" sites, such as battlegrounds, scenes of horrific crimes or acts of genocide.,

N. Social tourism

Social tourism is making tourism available to poor people who otherwise could not afford to travel for their education or recreation.

O. Doom tourism

This emerging trend involves traveling to places that are

environmentally or otherwise threatened.

P. DNA tourism

DNA tourism, also called "ancestry tourism" or "heritage travel", is tourism based on DNA testing. These tourists visit their remote relatives or places where their ancestors came from, or where their relatives reside, based on the results of DNA tests.

DIFFERENCES & REQUIREMENT-

TIRTH is a place where people travel for their better health and Auspicious Health.This is 100% disciplined and needs 100% disciplined activity.

This needs more area to be open with suitable Ashram to serve and create a Kshetra of Auspicious magnetic field.

People getting Energy even entering to Kshetra of TIRTH.

Tourism has to meet others, marketing for specific reasons etc.This totally depends on self interest and deeds.Hotel culture is only to stay and enjoy in their own way.

This is the right time to have discussion to understand that why Bolbam Tirth in Sawan, Bhado.We will discuss the same issue in Chapter-3

CHAPTER-4

Why is the Bolbam Tirth Extreme in Sawan, Bhado, Average in Asin & Karthik & Lower in other months?

Summary of Dosha and Season

Dosha	ChayaDosha (Accumulation of Dosha)	Prakopa (Excessive local accumulation)	Prashamana (Auto Pacification of Dosha)
VATA DOSHA	Greeshma (Summer)	Varsha (Rainy Season)	Sharath (Autumn)
PITTA DOSHA	Varsha (Rainy Season)	Sharath (Autumn)	Hemantha (Early Winter)
KAPHA DOSHA	Shishira (Winter)	Vasanta (Spring)	Greeshma (Summer)

Sawan, Bhado, Asin & Karthik is the month when there is prakopa of VATA DOSHA.

VATA Dosha is the key to all Dosha developing in the Human Body.

Hence Controlling of VATA Dosha showing a way to cure the other Dosha. Walking is a simple way to reduce the VATA DOSHA.

Continuous barefoot Walking in Satvik Condition escalates the sensitivity after Continuously developing the Frictional Force in Leg.

It creates a continuous vibration in the human body in a systematic way from bottom(Toe) to Top(Head) and develops an energy which burns the Extra Fat causing controlling of Cholesterol level causing control of BP,

Sugar level.

Rainfall and Muddy surface of the road in Rainy Season receive the all-fusion result: the whole body becomes light in a 110 km walk.

Law of Newton -

In the first law, an object will not change its motion or static in nature unless a force acts on it.

In the second law, the force on an object is equal to its mass times its acceleration.

In the third law, when two objects interact, they apply forces to each other of equal magnitude and opposite direction.

ACTION-

When Continuously walking barefoot it develops a frictional force in between leg and earth and the static condition of Human body is converting in movement.

Once movement takes place, force develops in the human body and continuous movement develops continuous Force causing Momentum in the Human body.

Momentum creates mechanical and electric energy in the human body while balancing the three dosha.

This force transfers to Earth as Legs directly connect to Earth and Earth force directly passes to the Human body.

As Earth is Muddy is much sensitive to receive Energy from Human body and transfer the energy to Human body, because percentage of water in human body is 72%, Earth-12%, Akash-6%Air-6% and Heat-4%.

The Energy (in the form of Mechanical and Electric energy) transfers from each other balancing the Five Elements and three Dosha.

Similarly when there is no waterfall and Hot Sunray reaches the Human body, Earth and Air is Hot increasing the Heat in the Human body causing burning of skin under Legs and it also causing defects in Eye and other sensory parts.

It also affects the Thigh area which is under Frictional Force.

If Bitumen, Concrete or else is the surface (Not suitable for Human body), it rubs the skin under Legs causing different types of heat formation trouble under Legs.

Even shoes or slippers also cause different types of heat formation in different parts of the body and trouble under Legs.

Hence Sawan, Bhado have heavy Rain means excellent month for movement, Asin and Kartik have little rain moderate for movement and rest of the month is dry-Walking is suitable only in the morning for a few hours and evening after cooling the Earth.

The mythology description of Samudra Manthan depicts churning of mind in meditation and subsequent release of negative thoughts. They can only be tackled by the release of positive thoughts (Ganges- a flow of positive thoughts) by the moon (cool mind).

Mythology tells the story of the ocean being churned by the *asura*s and *devas*, using the Mandara mountain range (in modern-day Cameroon), lassoed by the serpent king Vasuki. According to one version, the churning produced 14 different types of rubies, 13 of which were given to demons while one, Halahal, was given to Lord Shiva. Halahal was poisonous and turned Lord Shiva blue.This happened in the month of Sawan itself.The gods panicked and gave him water from the river Ganga to nullify the effects of the poison, and this worked, although he remained blue.

Scientific & Spiritual Significance

Shravan is the first month of Chaturmas which is the starting four months of Dakshinayana. In Uttarayana the days are longer and in Dakshinayana the nights are longer. Uttarayana is the period of positive state of the mind and Dakshinayana is the period of negative state of the mind. In the month of Shravan the mind is most unstable. As per Ayurveda it's a period of Vata imbalance. Main festivals to control the mind are held in this month starting from Guru Purnima, a day to go to your Guru to learn the ways for managing the negative mind in Chaturmas period.

Kanwar yatra is a spiritual journey of days, walking on foot, away from the routine stress, covering a long distance with a positive intent in the mind. It purifies the mind and continuous chanting (japa) helps in detoxifying the mind, body and soul. It works on the principle of incubation period for mental detoxification.

In spiritual language attachments, anger, greed, desires and ego are slow poisons representing Halahal of Lord Shiva.

One should not drink anger or spit anger but temporarily keep it in the throat and modify it when the opportunity arises. In mythology 'vish' is poison and 'vishay' is slow poison like negative thoughts.

Pouring gangajal to the halahala poison of Shiva indicates that we should calm down all anger or negative thoughts in our life if not routinely at least during the spiritual journeys cum retreats.

In mythology Brahma, Vishnu and Mahesh signifies the controllers of the start of a work, doing the work and completing the work respectively (creator, organizer and destroyer or winding up). Mahesh or Shiva therefore is the controller of any work which needs winding up. If any task is not getting completed we worship Lord Shiva for guidance.

When the churning of oceans - Samudra Manthan - took place in the month of Shravan, fourteen different types of rubies came out. Thirteen of these were distributed amongst the demons, except Halahal (poison). Lord Shiva drank the Halahal and stored it in his throat. Hence the name Neelkantha (meaning blue throat) is attributed to Shiva. To reduce the strong effect of poison, Lord Shiva wore the crescent moon on his head. All the Gods thereafter started offering the Ganges water to Lord Shiva to lessen the effect of poison. Since, this happened in the month of Shravan, since then the Shiva devotees offer the Ganges water in this month.

When we take our car for a long distance we first get its servicing done. Same way we must have a clearance from the doctor before undertaking this yatra.

Lord Parsuram was the First Bolbam Tirth Yatri who took Water from Sultanganj and poured the Water to Deoghar Shivling.

Lord Ram, Sita and Laxman scoop up water from the Ganga at Sultanganj and walk to the *shivling* in Deoghar.

Pilgrims from as far away as Nepal and all corners of India now follow in these footsteps, picking up the water from Sultanganj and walking 108 kilometers barefoot all the way to Deoghar to pour the water on the *shivling* , chanting 'Bol Bam' all the way.

Lets understand the meaning of Uttaryani Ganga Jal.in next chapter.

CHAPTER-5

Why Uttarayani Ganga Jal?

The term *Uttarvahini Ganga* is used to refer to places where the Ganges river has a northward flow.

For the majority of its route, the Ganges flows in a generally southeasterly direction, from the Himalaya mountains in western Nepal to its delta emptying into the Bay of Bengal. However, there are several places where the meandering of the river leads to a northerly flow, which is considered auspicious.

Reason-

In India Uttarvahini is auspicious because -

Morning air flowing through North to South or North-East to South-West and East to West.

90% of the above air is blowing in North -East area.

River Uttar Vahini means when air touches to blow it gets more water content due to downward to upward flow that increases the oxygen in air.

In Morning sun rays directly touch the flow of the river which creates Energy as flow is downward to upward flow.

Hence water in Uttar Vahini has more oxygen content than regular flow of river.

Taking a dip in the Ganga River in morning is very auspicious to receive the oxidant and light refraction energy and Gangajal is more energetic.

Hence Uttar Vahini Gangajal in morning is very auspicious.

Significant places of *Uttarvahini Ganga*

Uttarakhand

Haridwar

Haridwar is a holy place for Hindus. 'Hari' terms belong to Lord Vishnu and 'Dwar' represents doors. Also known as Hari Dham. Here Ganga is *Uttarayan* for a little.

Uttar Pradesh

Kashi

In Kashi, the Ganges has a more distinct northerly flow than at Haridwar. The Ganges here merges with five more rivers like Varuna and Assi. which is why this place is also known as Varanasii. It is said that Kashi is set on the Trishul of Lord Shiva.

Bhrigu Thaura

In Bhrigu Thaura, the Ganges has a more distinct northerly flow than at Haridwar.

Bihar

Barh

Barh, a city in Patna district located on the bank of Uttar Vahini Ganga. One of the holiest & historic temples of Hindu of Lord Shiva also known as UMANATH located on the bank of Uttar Vahini Ganga. The temple is the famous spot of pilgrimage of locals in Sawan month. People came over here from different places to put Gangajal in sawan month over shivling.

Simaria (Begusarai)-

This place is located in Begusarai District.People taking dip on Puranmashi, Amavasya and all auspicious day. People collecting the Energies Gangajal and barefoot walking to Indradamnehwar dham(Ashokdham, Lakhisarai)-Kageshwar dham(Jamui)-Deoghar.

Barhiya-

Located in Lakhisarai District.People taking dip on Puranmashi,

Amavasya and all auspicious day .People collecting the Energies Gangajal and barefoot walking to Indradamnehwar dham(Ashokdham)-Kageshwar dham(Jamui)-Devghar.

Indradamneshwar dham which is always open 24x7x365 days for Mundan, Janew, Marriage.

The Maa Parvati temple is tied up with the main temple, with huge red sacred threads which is unique and worthy of reverence, showing the unity of Shiva and Shakti. According to the stories narrated in the Shiva Purana, the holy Baidyanath temple resembles the unity of souls and thus fits marriage for Hindus.

Bhagalpur

The Uttarvahini Ganga's impact in the Bhagalpur region has effects on Sultanganj and kahalgaon, which plays a pivotal role in the spiritual culture of this ancient city. Bhagalpur has been culturally rich and a center of religion, culture, education, trade etc. from ancient times.

Sultanganj

In Sultanganj, Ganga is in uttar vahini for almost half kilometers, where the holy Ajgaivinath Temple is situated. Every year during the holy month of Sawan, millions of devotees of Lord Shiva take the water of the holy river as 'Ganga Jal' to 110 km from here to Baba Baidyanath Dham or Baidyanath Temple, for the 'Jal Abhishek'.

Kahalgaon

Here the Ganges covers a long distance as Uttarvahini for 6 kilometers. From Kahalgaon to Bateshwar Sthan, the Ganges is completely *Uttar Vahini*. Here the Koshi and Ganges rivers merge, where Maharishi Vashistha is believed to have worshiped. Identifying the importance of this place, in the 8th century, King Dharampal of Pal Dynasty, formed the

World famous Vikramshila Mahavihara in this place.

We will understand the Morning Dip in Uttarayani Ganga in the next chapter.

Why Morning Dip in Uttarayani Ganga?

Morning air flowing through North to South or North-East to South-West and East to West.

90% of the above air is blowing in the North -East area.

River Uttar Vahini means when air touches to blow it gets more water content due to downward to upward flow that increases the oxygen in air.

In Morning sun rays directly touch the flow of the river which creates Energy as flow is downward to upward flow.

In Afternoon sun rays inclindly touch the flow of river which creates Energy. (Minimum) as flow is upward to downward flow.

In Evening sun rays directly touch the flow of the river which creates Energy (Minimum) as flow is upward to downward flow.

Hence water in Uttar Vahini has more oxygen content than regular flow of river.

Taking a dip in the Ganga River in morning is very auspicious to receive the oxidant and light refraction energy and Gangajal is more energetic.

Hence Uttar Vahini Gangajal in morning is very auspicious.

This is now time to understand the technology of Barefoot walking on Earth 110km in next chapter.

Why Barefoot Walking on Earth 110 km?

We are missing the transfer of energy from earth to the human body, once we are in Chappal or Shoe, because once leg not touching the Earth is creating a GAP, while energy of shoe and chappal we are gaining after walking.

Kharau (A Chappal of Wood) was used in ancient times to get energy from Wood and humans are getting the energy of wood in place of Earth. While long journey was barefoot only.

Leg should not get infected by surrounding dirtiest thing. People started using Chappal and shoes and now it is a fashion. Those who are barefoot are called poor, poor.

Details of technology is described below-

Inflammation has been widely recognised as the leading trigger of chronic pain and many major health disorders from cardiovascular disease, diabetes and arthritis to some forms of cancer. It has been mooted that all paths to chronic disease lead through inflammation and an informative question is ``If all roads lead to inflammation, how do we get healthy?''

In short, inflammation is a reaction of our immune system to intruders – bacteria, viruses and foreign bodies such as pollen and air pollutants.

An inflammatory response is required to fight off common colds and allergies, but chronic inflammation that can occur in the aftermath of inflammation can take its toll on our healthy cells as white blood cells flood to the area 'leaving healthy cells stressed and overwrought'. Many diseases can be aside from barefoot walking, there are a number of ways to ground and each focuses on reconnecting yourself to the earth either through direct or indirect contact traced back to chronic inflammation.

Lying on the ground

Increasing body to earth contact by lying in the grass or on the sand is an easy way to ground.

INSIGHTS FOR BAREFOOT TECHNOLOGY-

Barefoot Walking is not a seasonal exercise, rather a year-round therapeutic technique that reconnects us electrically to the earth in order to ground.

Walking barefoot have a positive influence on health?

This is because the negative ions present in the earth balance out the positive ions present inside yourself, creating a balance that will give you improved health. When walking barefoot, the pressure points on your feet get activated and give your body energy.

Barefoot walking yielded **greater medio lateral COP displacement, flatter foot contact angle, increased ankle plantar flexion contact angle, and smaller knee flexion contact angle and range of motion** compared to all other footwear.

Barefoot walking has been shown to help increase antioxidants, reduce inflammation and improve sleep.

WHEN WE MAKE A CONNECTION WITH THE EARTH, WHEN WE GROUND THROUGH BAREFOOT WALKING, THERE HAS BEEN FOUND TO BE A REDUCTION IN WHITE BLOOD CELLS AND AN INCREASE IN RED BLOOD CELLS, WHICH HINTS TO BETTER IMMUNITY.

Throw off our shoes and enjoy the grounding effect of the grass beneath our feet as we enjoy the Estate and find a space to rest, reset and restore.

What is grounding?

Grounding is simple and easy.

What could be more connective than walking barefoot on the earth?

Our world is full of magnetic forces and electromagnetic waves that are not in alignment with our own energetic field.

Think phone, electricity, microwaves and smart meters.

There is strong evidence to suggest that these electromagnetic waves, which affect our own sensitive frequency, can make us ill.

Walking or standing on the earth for at least 30 minutes seems to have very powerful healing potential.

Damp grass and sand are the best surfaces.

The earth carries a huge negative charge within it, which is electron rich and acts as a powerful antioxidant, helping to remove free radicals from the body. We are part of nature and nature is part of us, so there is no surprise that walking directly on the earth helps our own energy to flow more freely.

In our busy, stressful lives the simple action of taking off our shoes and feeling the grass beneath our feet must also be a great stress reliever.

Walking barefoot is considered therapeutic. Internet results, in fact, show that walking barefoot on the ground helps one absorb all the negative charge from the earth through our feet into the body.

'Earthing' or 'grounding' works when our body is in direct contact with earth, making an electrical connection with its energies.

Nature-immersive wellness practices have proved beneficial for many.

Late painter MF Husain, in fact, walked barefoot all his life.

"Everyone needs grounding.

One of the most profound forms of grounding is to walk or sit on the bare ground with no shoes or socks, and to touch and connect with the soil or earth.

Activities like playing with soil, building sand castles on the beach, etc, help in fighting sadness, anxiety and depression, besides having other positive effects.

The easiest perhaps is just to walk on the (non-carpeted) floor at home or sit on it.

Grounding helps in maintaining the health of the root chakra, the first chakra of the seven main chakras in the body, which is based on the earth element.

It's responsible for confidence, support, the musculoskeletal system and sustenance.

"When we lose our connection with earth, we find ourselves in a mental flurry or feeling floaty, drifty, disconnected and unsettled, " adding that the mind, body and soul are interdependent on earth.

Any healing to one will affect the other two.

Grounding can reduce stress levels, help the body recover from stress-induced issues and uplift the spirit.

Playing with soil is a powerful lifestyle change and makes one's immunity strong.

"Get our children to play in the mud and soil because the microbes in them get into their fingernails, skin and they reach their gut, making the gut as well as their immunity extremely strong.

A healthy gut is everything when it comes to immunity, assimilation and digestion.

Handling soil also improves the ratio of good bacteria versus bad bacteria, making our immunity grow stronger.

This is how we enable the body to help prevent allergies and possibly heal them.

If we have a limitation on space, invest in building a microbiome or mud box.

It contains organic soil and a few leaves… We can play with the soil for 5 minutes.

It is therapeutic; it connects us with nature.

Modern lifestyles have, however, distanced us from nature, and this may have been aggravated by the current health crisis, which is forcing us all to stay indoors.

"Grounding may be an under-researched area compared to other therapies in modern medicine… But earthing is different from grounding techniques used by mental health professionals to help treat people from stressful experiences and reorient their senses to be mindful in the present moment.

The surface of the earth has ample free electrons that are taken up by our body on direct skin contact—think of this as nature's biggest and most freely available antioxidant.

It is basic conduction that neutralizes excess free radicals that could be otherwise damaging to our body.

Grounding not only has several physiological benefits—reducing inflammation and wound healing, preventing and treating auto immune conditions, and improving sleep problems and chronic pain—but also enhances general well-being.

"The mind-body connection is undeniable, as is this technique's direct effect on reducing stress and improving mood.

The most amazing thing is the accessibility of this health practice.

It's as simple as walking barefoot on grass.

We can also make a more conscious effort by lying down in nature or wading through a natural water body, which can work in a similar way.

HEALTH BENEFITS OF WALKING BAREFOOT

There are many health benefits to our body if we walk barefoot. Here are a few below:

1. It Can Control Insomnia

We have trouble sleeping at night and often find ourselves sleepless even till the wee hours of the morning, we may be suffering from sleeplessness or insomnia which is a type of sleep disorder.

We are unable to sleep well, so instead of taking sleeping pills, try walking in the park.

We will see a stark difference in our sleeping pattern from day one.

But to prevent insomnia or improve our sleeping patterns, try walking barefoot on grass for around 30-minute every morning.

It is believed that one of the benefits of walking barefoot on grass is that our insomnia can be cured.

2. Improves Eyesight

There is a pressure point on our feet which is believed to be connected to the nerves of our eye.

Well, according to the science of reflexology, when we walk, we put maximum pressure on our second and third toe.

These two have the maximum nerve endings, which stimulate the functioning of our eyes.

Hence, walking barefoot on grass also keeps our vision in check.

Walking barefoot can stimulate this pressure point and help improve our overall eyesight.

3. The Nervous System can be Improved

Walking barefoot at home can stimulate specific acupuncture points in the foot, and this will, in turn, stimulate our nerves and veins, thereby improving our nervous system.

Diabetic people who experience pain from varicose veins can relieve it if we walk barefoot on a regular basis.

4. Immunity can be Increased

Children love to play around barefoot. Since walking barefoot stimulates the nervous system, it also helps in increasing one's immunity by making one stronger and less susceptible to disorder.

5. Increases Energy

One of the benefits of walking barefoot on sand is that it gives us resistance and this stimulates the pressure points on our feet.

We may find it difficult to walk on the sand for a few days, but as our feet get used to it, we will develop more strength in our legs and body.

Our energy level will increase and keep us active during the day. We get the same benefits by walking barefoot on pebbles or barefoot on stones.

6. Helps Menstrual and Hormonal Issues

When our hormones are not in balance, we will experience physical and mental problems. Women who have premenstrual syndrome often have mood swings, headaches, stomach pain, a gain in weight, acne, constipation, and other issues. Walking barefoot on the ground can help ease many of these symptoms.

7. Reduces Inflammation

Inflammation is caused by damage to our body's cells, which may lead to complications like cancer, aging, heart issues, and other problems.

Walking barefoot on grass helps to stimulate the functioning of our organs. Now this can be multi-fold.

One is due to reflexology.

Second, we are bathing in morning sunlight and getting vitamin D, which is known for its anti-inflammatory properties.

Lastly, it is because of the electrons of the earth's magnetic field.

Walking barefoot helps the electrons in the ground act as antioxidants and reduce inflammation in our body.

8. Cardiovascular Activity is Improved

Walking barefoot helps improve the nervous system.

Walking barefoot on grass helps to synchronize our heart beat.

And why is it important?

Because from regulating our body temperature to hormone secretion, everything depends on it. Plus, our heart health also remains in check, as the other organs of the body function well.

This, in turn, helps improve blood circulation in our body.

More blood circulation means a healthier cardiovascular system.

9. Maintains Blood Pressure

Our stress levels automatically come down when we walk barefoot as the nerves in our feet are stimulated, releasing stress.

This is similar to when we get a foot reflexology massage. Since our stress comes down, our blood pressure also gets stable.

10. It Clears our Mind and Improves Mood

We have a lot of internal chatter going on in our head and suffer from mood swings. Walking barefoot in snow or on the grass can help us relax and focus on the present.

Psychological benefits of taking a walk in the park, and if we do it barefoot, then there is a lot more to be thankful about.

Our body absorbs negative electrons through the earth which helps create within it a balanced bio-electrical environment.

Understanding of BOLBAM Mantra is equally important to discuss in the next chapter.

CHAPTER-8

Why is the BOLBAM Mantra chanted?

Mantras have their own sound, which affect the human body.Every word has sense and meaning separately.

Respiration-Respiration is the starting of Mantra.Once respiration starts mantra is started.

AUM-

Think when nothing to talk means when mouth is opening and shutting there are three primary words developed is aaaa. Auuu. mmm means AUM .

This is the first word or mantra of the whole world.This word dispels the respiration to akash.

Means-

We are respiring from the nose, it reaches to lungs and attaches in biological activity to run the human.

When mouth opens the first word Aaaa is starting from kanth auuu from talu and mmm from hote.Its direction is from inner to outer Akash.Vibration is similar to nature gives peace to body.

BOLBAM-

Similarly Bolbam is similar. This AUM is changing to Bolbam due to use of tongue but vibration is similar and matching with vibration of nature and direction is upward.

Once sound is upward to akash concentration increasing like nature and the human body becoming stronger, it can sustain any force or energy.

Respiration is the reason of Strength.Oncr strength reached in body Vata, Pitta and Kapha Dosha developing inside (Tantra)

It comes out from the external part of the body by (Yantra), Similarly much Vata energy comes out from the mouth in the form of different sounds.

Sound which comes outward in line of Akash clearing the body from other Dosha.Its vibration is matching with vibration of nature.

Respiration-Sound-Inner Dosha/Energy-Man-Budhi-Ego

Respiration itself creates Energy , Sound.This affects the Man Budhi and Ego in the Human body.

Sound which developed inward it's vibration is different from natural vibration.This acts differently to Human body.It increases the three Dosha causing ill affect.

This is observed that vibration matching to nature and upward to akash is powerful means when similar vibration continues for a long time mind shifting from the human body and body attaching to nature such that Budhi and Ego attach to nature and gain auspicious energy and get extraordinary strength.

Similarly BOLBAM creates a vibration which is matching to vibration of Nature and direction is outward upward to Akash and very effective to Chant.

This is observed that the Name who is chanting Bolbam for 120km barefoot walk gaining extreme energy even the same Bam getting extra energy to watch long and faraway.

This is also observed that trouble arising inside the human body is settling down and three Dosha and five elements equalize.

Application of BOLBAM-

Mantra means a sound, a certain utterance or a syllable. Today, modern science sees the whole existence as reverberations of energy, different levels of vibrations. Where there is a vibration, there is bound to be a sound. So, that means, the whole existence is a kind of sound, or a complex amalgamation of soundz – the whole existence is an amalgamation of multiple mantras. Of these, a few mantras or a few sounds have been identified, which could be like keys. If we use them in a certain way, they become a key to open up a different dimension of life and experience within self.

Significance of Bol Bam

'Bol Bam' is said to be an efficacious mantra. When it is chanted on the way to a temple, **it generates energy and enthusiasm among the kanwarias and gives them the strength to carry on walking a long distance**.

BOLBAM means Shiva

According to the Skanda Purana, those who complete the holy journey by reciting Bam-Bam obtain the virtues of Ashwamedha Yajna (the one done to control the senses).

Scientifically any chanting, which ends with a nasal consonant (MMMMMM) produces tranquility of the mind by producing delta activity in the EEG. These are also weeping sounds.

BOL BAM

This auspicious word has a very deep sense. Bam means Brahma that further means brahmaand, The overall sristi whatever is saakar/sagun or nirakar/nirgun. Then other bam means naad (sound the energy present in). So the meaning of "BOL BAM " is "Bhole the Lord shiva, is present in overall brahmand in the form of energy Naad

Aumkaar. He is the most powerful, God of gods, but even then he is very Calm, Nirmal, shaant BHOLA.

Nada Yoga – The Link Between Sound and Form

The Sanskrit language is a device, not necessarily a medium of communication. Most of the other languages were made up because we had to refer to something. Initially, they started with just a handful of words and then multiplied them into complex forms. But Sanskrit is a discovered language because today we know that if you feed any sound into an oscilloscope, every sound has a form attached to it. Similarly, every form has a sound attached to it. Every form in existence is reverberating in a certain way and creates a certain sound.

When you utter a sound, a form is being created. There is a whole science of using sounds in a particular way so that it creates the right kind of form. We can create powerful forms by uttering sounds in certain arrangements. This is known as the Nada Yoga, the yoga of sound. If you have mastery over the sound you also have mastery over the form that is attached to it.

When Sanskrit is taught, it has to be learnt by rote. The sound is important, not the meaning.

The sound is the criteria. When you realize what sound is attached to a particular form, you give this sound as the name for that form. Now the sound and the form are connected. If you utter the sound, you are relating to the form – not just psychologically, but existentially, you are connecting with the form. Sanskrit is like a blueprint of existence. What is in form, we converted into sound. A lot of distortions have happened. How to preserve it in its right form has become a challenge even today since the necessary knowledge, understanding, and awareness is largely missing.

Sound is More Important than Meaning

That is the reason why when Sanskrit is taught, it has to be learnt by rote. People just chant the language endlessly. It does not matter whether you know the meaning or not. The sound is important, not the meaning. Meanings are made up in your mind. It is the sound and the form which are connecting. Are you connecting or not? – That is the question. That is why it has become the mother of almost all Indian and European languages, except Tamil. Tamil did not come from Sanskrit. It developed independently. All the other Indian languages and almost all the European languages have their origin in sanskrit..

Mantra is not consciousness but mantra sets the right kind of ambience. Sound will set the right kind of ambience within this physiological, psychological framework and also in the atmosphere.

Let us talk about how Barefoot walking purifies the Body in the next talk.

CHAPTER-9

How does Barefoot walking activity Purify the Body?

Question is arised what purification means.

Once again the answer is similar.

List of all we'll understand the Equilibrium of five elements.

Nature and Human is the combination of

Akash-   6%,

Air- 6%,

Heat-4%,

Water-   72% and

Earth-   12%

It creates three Dosha is under-

Combination of Akash and Air is VATA Dosha.

Combination of Heat and Water is PITTA Dosha.

Combination of Water and Earth is KAPHA Dosha.

Combination of VATA-PITTA-KAPHA is the reason of MARNASAN

Nature and Human body self control the all three Dosha.

Deflection in Dosha creates trouble in Nature and the Human body.

Balancing Dosha is the natural procedure.

In summer heat is generated in nature similarly in Human body.We are controlling heat to not move outside keeping Towel or Cap on head.Nature is controlling to have grass on Earth.

Once heat increasing in Human body heat stroke, cold cough trouble comes in human body.Pitta trouble generating in human body.similarly in nature cracks developing in Earth and when it rain falling vaporizing takes place in Nature.Fruits, Vegetable becomes toxic.Heat disturbing the air causing Heat Vata Dosha due to heat Air+Akash

In the rainy season once water percentage increases means formation of new creatures, flood takes place in nature, which affects the human body in form of different types of fever and reaction in human body due to increase of water.Earth percentage reduces causing disturbance in Kapha Dosha.

Moisturized Air+Akash disturbing the Vata Dosha.

In Winter season again heat reduces and water content increases in nature and similarly in the human body.Pitta Dosha unbalancing.

Foggy Air+Akash disturbing the Vata Dosha.

In the Junction of two seasons Dosha is disturbing in nature and human also.

Summer-Rainy

Vata+Pitta Dosha is common in nature and humans due to heat and water.

Rainy+Winter

Vata+Kapha Dosha is common in nature and humans due to water and Earth.

Winter+Summer

Vata+Pitta Dosha is common in nature and humans due to moisture and heat.

Balancing Dosha needs different types of activity in routine such as walking, yoga posture, Meditation, work, Food and Movement as per different climate and nature.

PURIFICATION-

Various methods to Purify the Human body are as under.

1. Continuously Barefoot Walking of 100 km on Earth from (Sawan-Bhado-Asin-Karthik and other month)

2. Continuous Meditation for 11 days.

3. Pancha Kriya and Meditation for 11 days.(Oil Massage-2hr morning evening, Nasya-Taking oil in nose one time, Virechan Kriya-Inner oilation-Eating khichdi & Ghee five day, Pugation kriya- 2 days-Cleaning of Colon, Rakta Cleaning by donation of Rakta.) and rest period is for Meditation for mental peace.

4. Continuously Group Chanting of Mantra for 30-180 days with auspicious dance.

(Ex-Hare Krishna, Hare Krishna, Krishna, Krishna, Hare Hare.Hare Rama, Hare Rama, Rama, Rama, Hare, Hare.)

5. Sanyas-Leave the home without any greed or attachment.OR perform SEVA without attachment.

All methods need to follow common steps as below.

1.Wake up in the morning at 4am.

2.Vaishnav Breakfast-6.30am to 7.00am

3.Vaishnav Lunch-11.00am to 11.30am

4.Vaishnav Light Dinner-6pm to 7pm

Barefoot Walking of 100km on Earth from(Sawan-Bhado-Asin-Karthik and other months)is one of the ways to equalize the five elements and three Dosha.

Restricting walking in the heat condition of nature means no rainfall means Earth and Air both becoming hot.

1. Touching of Earth continuously equalizes the Earth Element.

2. Whole body is open to equalize the Akash element.

3. Regular Bathing or rain bath equalizing the water element.

4. Movement generating the heat through Frictional Force between Leg and Earth, which destroys the freezed element in joints and equalizes the Heat element.

5. Continuous walking on Earth creates heat which equalizes the Vata element from Human body.

As per experience this activity starts after continuous movement of 12 hours itself and purifies the whole body in movement of 110km.

Getting support in the way of walking is extraordinary to understand and is now in position to talk.

CHAPTER-10

How Self Dependent Business is Developing with Innovative Ideas?

Self dependent business is developing as per requirement of the locality, society, tirth etc .

What innovative ideas should come out from the BOLBAM Tirth.

Let us discuss.

1. Cloth suitability is Light either white or Violet color or color of sun in half pants and light tee shirt or ganji.Underwear is not suitable.Dhoti is recommended but difficult to maintain.

2. Garland purse is necessary to wear in the neck to keep mobile and money in safe condition.

3. One bag is required to be kept on one shoulder with one set of cloth, sleeping plastic and chadar.

4. kamar is required which will carry the 3 gangajal drums hinged with thread.

5. Puja material such as arwa rice, kaseli, pan, ganga soil, agarbatti, flower, machis etc and Panda is required to Abhimantrit the Ganga JAL.

6. Bathing place with shower to regularly bathe after disposal of urine and latrine.Morning toilet and bathing facility.

7. Hot water, ayurvedic oil to rub in the leg.

8. Frequent line hotel with facility of wooden bed, wooden bed sleeping facility with fan, drinking water, tea, coffee, milk, peda, sweets, fruits like Banana, Apple, Mango, Pomegranate, Grape etc.

Hotel also have facility of Nasta, Lunch and Dinner for whom who is not in fruit fasting.

9. Some Bam got injured and needs a medical facility.

10. Few Bam lost the energy to run needs facility of vehicles to reach shivling.

11. Dharmshala is also required where needy BAM take rest drinking Bhang and Ganja and enjoying the Shiva chanting, Shiva Sangeet.

12. Ashram is required to stay in Tirth place, where Bam can prepare the food and enjoy the Tirth.

13. Panda is required to abhi mantrit the JAL before pouring on shivling with flower, pan etc.

14. Bam is purchasing different Prasad like Sweets, Badhi, Bangal, Bindi and other Ladies beauty items.

15. Road quality should be such that human barefoot should feel comfort.Green Road is a real solution.

16. Green Road should have a facility of greenery, water pouring, solar panel for solar lighting, borewell and shower.

Following Innovative business continuing beside the BOLBAM Tirth path is as under-

1. Cloth factory and Market to prepare and sell the Dhoti, Belt with pocket, Half pant, T-shirt, Ganjee, Air bag, Plastic bed sheet, Covering bed sheet, Garland with Bag to keep the mobile and money safely before reaching to Ganga River or River.

2. Plantation of Bamboo, preparation and selling of Kambar, Thread, Plastic pots, Metal pots before reaching the Ganga River or River.

3. Ashram with suitable Fooding arrangement for both fasting and non fasting Bam is required near Ganga River such that Bam should stay in evening and morning after dip in Ganga can move to Tirth with Gangajal

on Kambar.

4. At Ganga Ghat, there is requirement of urinal and latrine such that cleaning should be ensured before taking DIP in Ganga River.

5. Plantation of flower, pan, kaseli is required and selling at Ganga Ghat is required to fulfill the need of BAM.

6. Production of Puja items such as agarbatti, Machis and ganga mud is required and selling point needed on Gangaghat.

7. Production of Apple, Banana, Orange, Lemon, Grape, Mango, Guava and various selling points needed.

8. Production of bottling water, Milk, various fresh juice and various selling points needed.

9. Production of wooden bed, wooden bed sleeping facility with fan and opening of Line hotel with facility of Borewell, Spring, Toilet etc and facility of food for fasting and non fasting Bam.

10. Production of health products such as Medicine, Cotton, Ayurvedic oil, Hot water and facility on Bolbam Path.

11. Production of vehicle and arrangement to bring the Unhealthy BAM to Tirth.

12. Production of Pera, Prasad, Bengal, Bindi, Nail polish, kajal, Lipstick and other Ladies beauty item, cloth, T-Shirt, Saree, Dhoti, Local Sweets, Local product like Bhavra and various selling points to sell and transfer the culture.

13. Development of University & Research Center beside Tirth to study and provide a platform to offer degrees to the public on the BOLBAM Tirth from Nursery to PHD.

14. Development of 10000 sqft.Green area, Ashram, Park, Green Road, with green solar lighting, various Borebell, plenty of Spring to take bath

beside Shiva Lingam temple.Due to increase of population pond bath is not recommended, but ponds should be developed surrounding with various Borebell, spring, solar green lighting, park with green road and greenery.

15. Manufacturing of Bus, Auto, Car, Air Car, Tram and Development of Bus Depot, Auto Depot, Car Depot, Airport, Surrounding Tram line should developed at both place, where BAM taken dip in Ganga River/River and Place of Tirth of Shivalingam.

16. Development of Health center beside the surrounding of Tirth and Cremation center away the surrounding of Tirth.

17. Development of TIRTH DEVELOPMENT CENTER to control the all activity.

Let's talk and understand how the Bolbam Yatra became much Effective.

CHAPTER-11

How will the Bolbam Yatra become much Effective?

Bol Bam yatra is a Barefoot walk from River to Shivalingam.

This Yatra is an Yatra which is attached with the Nature.Taking dip in Ganga, collecting Abhimantrit uttarayan jal and barefoot walking to Shivalingam to pour.There is two fusion takes place.Once when BAM walking barefoot, the human percentage of jal have fusion with Gangajal and secondly when jal poured to Shivalingam it again have fusion which creates Energy benefitting to Human.

Barefoot Yatra is a Natural Yatra, hence the following facility should make an effective Yatra.

1. Barefoot have comfort with Earth, hence Bitumen Road, Concrete Road should be avoided or if any road has to be dismantled and Green Road has to be constructed.

2. Green Road with Ganga silt has comfort to BAM.Hence similar road has to be constructed.

3. Frequent toilet and bathing is the essential requirement of BAM, hence provision of toilet, Borebell with spring will help the BAM.

4. Line hotel, Dharamshala with facility of wooden bed, wooden bed with fan facility to sleep and fasting and non fasting food facility will enrich the facility.

5. Solar lighting both sides, tree both sides, health center both sides, juice center will enrich the facility.

To create this effectively this is essential to understand the meaning of

GREEN Road.Let's talk.

CHAPTER-12

Why Green Road?

Bolbam Yatra starts from Dip in Ganga River/River collecting jal and starting barefoot yatra or Sastang yatra.

Roads have a major role in Yatra. Quality and cleaning of roads is a serious concern.

Various of road is in use of BOLBAM Yatra details of technical aspect is as under.-

1. Bituminous Road- is a common Road.This is the combination of Bitumen, aggregate.

Bitumen and aggregate is unsuitable for the Barefoot and Sastang, hence there are chances of rubbing of barefoot and human body.

In hot weather this road is unsuitable for Barefoot and Sastang there are chances of burning of Barefoot and human body similarly in rainy season water creating gap between the aggregate which rubs the barefoot and human body.

2. Concrete Road- is also a common road mainly in towns and in villages.

Concrete itself is unsuitable for Barefoot and human for sastang.hence there are chances of rubbing of barefoot and human body.

In hot weather this road is unsuitable for Barefoot and Sastang. There are chances of burning of Barefoot and human body similarly in rainy season water creating a gap between the aggregate which rubs the barefoot and human body.

3. Paver Block Road- Paver Block is prepared by cement aggregate and sand again it is not suitable in summer season and in rainy season.In summer it heat the barefoot and human body and it rub the barefoot and human body and in rainy season it will become the cause of rub the barefoot and human body.

4. Tiles- Footpath/Parking/Checkered- Tiles prepared by the cement, aggregate, sand and coloured.Base is hard and similar like paver block not suitable for barefoot walking and Sastang yatra.

5. Aggregate/WMM/GSB Road- This road is of aggregate itself is unsuitable for barefoot and Sastang yatra.This road creating pain in Leg.

6. Moorum/Gravel Road-Moorum. Moorum is also a type of soil, mostly used for construction purposes. Generally, it is deep brown or red in color. Moorum is used in plinth filling, road pavements, backfilling in trenches, footing pits, etc.

This is also one of the Green Road Material.

Moorum or Gravel Road with a layer of dust creates the Green Road.

Defect is that in the rainy season moorum is dislodged and creates a little tough road for the barefoot.Normally material availability in Hilly area.

Maintenance of this road is a regular activity.

7. Soil Road- Soil Road in the rainy season becomes slippery in the Rainy Season, hence this road is Green when grass is on or in dry condition.

Maintenance of this road is a regular activity.

8. Ganga Soil/Silt Road- Ganga Soil/Silt Road never becomes slippery in the rainy season.Ganga Soil/Silt contains much oxidant.This road is good for barefoot and satsang walk.Grass built up in this road in rainy season.

Maintenance of this road is a regular activity.

Hence Green Road is a Road which comfort to Barefoot, Sastang BAM or normal Yatri who moves without shoe or Chappal.A Road is suitable for barefoot, comfort to Barefoot, easy to Barefoot.Best suitable Green Road is built up by GANGA SOIL/SILT which is suitable in all season and its property is it have better oxidant after regular maintenance of the Road.

Now we have reached to understand the subject Bolbam Tirth & Green Road Concept.We will discuss in next session.

CHAPTER-13

What is the Bolbam Tirth & Green Road Concept?

BOLBAM TIRTH-

Collecting Uttarayani Ganga Jal, keeping in Kanwar or on Back, Barefoot Walking, Dak Bam, Sastang Walking with Jal, Chanting of Bolbam Mantra and Pouring on Shivling is the Bolbam Tirth.

Economy starts once two humans meet each other, each one is the source of the economy of the other. When traveling, meeting with different different humans means searching for the source of the economy.

Barefoot walking is a practical class in between the human body to learn Complete physics, chemistry, biology, Engineering, Medicine and economics.

CONCEPT OF GREEN ROAD

In simple words, GREEN ROAD is a Road which should be friendly of Nature or Road which does not disturb the Nature Quality such that there are no disturbances in ETHER, AIR, HEAT, WATER, EARTH, FOOD and ENVIRONMENT.

A green Road is a roadway constructed with a new concept for roadway design that integrates transportation functionality and ecological sustainability. An environmental approach is used throughout the planning, design, and the construction. The result is a Road that will benefit Public health, Health to Surrounding Communities, the ecosystem, urban growth, and Transportation.

Human and barefoot walking is the practice from the year when humans are born.Society developed Walking moved to transport, but barefoot walking is still alive culture as it has direct relation with Human body.

Science mainly physics, Chemistry, Biology, Sociology, psychology Engineering means Architecture, Civil Engineering, Electrical, Electronics, Mechanical, Chemical, Computer Medical means-Ayurveda, Allopathy, Homeopathy, Naturopathy is solely dependent on Human body and Nature.

When Barefoot movement or SASTANG MOVEMENT takes place, the human body gets a MOTION starting from foot to head.FRICTION developing in Foot.ENERGY transferring from foot to Earth.

Once BAREFOOT Movement or SASTANG MOVEMENT to 110km in JUNGLE, CITY, VILLAGE it teaching the

Solution of Three Law of Newton resolved.Static position is the FIRST LAW.Movement position MOMENTUM is the IIND LAW and THIRD LAW for every action there is reaction.

OSCILLATION work in hand.

HEAT is developing in movement of blood.PURIFICATION takes place due to increase in blood movement.Blood movement creating the OXIDATION.

Oxidation purifies the HEART, BLOCKAGE, BLOOD CLOTTING, URINARY, COLON. LIVER, BRAIN and all other ORGAN.Complete Medical science should be understood.

Organic and inorganic reactions take place in Human body.

Self food preparation takes place inside the Human body and we are awaying from hunger.

Reaction takes place and sleeping quality goes off.

Green Road, which has a green or cool or watery surface reacts with

Barefoot and energies the eye, causing increase of Eye sight, even spectacle coming out from the EYE.

Same time once Road is Bituminous, Concrete, Paver Block, Tiles, aggregate, Gravel in hot condition decreasing the EYE sight and in watery condition rub the foot, in cool condition similar energy transferring to human body causing a different energy developing in Human body, which come out as per newton Third Law.

It increases the sense and sense attaching the sense away from the place it is an ELECTRONICS and COMPUTER SCIENCE.

Movement reaching to Village or Town or City have a special sense of understanding of SOCIOLOGY and PSYCHOLOGY comes under the understanding.

REQUIREMENT-

BAREFOOT WALKING is the Ist requirement of the Society.

BULLOCK CART, HORSE CART is developed to carry material from one place to another place.

Humans discovered BICYCLES for fast movement and it has become a requirement.

Bicycles discovery creates the Path of MOTOR BIKES and it has further become the daily Requirement.

CARS are developed for Comfortable Journey and it is the requirement of each individual.

TRACTOR is developed for agriculture purposes and carries the materials from Land to Home and Home to Land.

TRUCK is developed for the movement of material from one place to other places.

BUS is developed to carry a group of people from one place to another place.

TRAM is an innovative car which has a feeling of roadway and trainway.

TRAM discovery creates the Path of TRAIN and it has further become the Daily Requirement.

BOAT is a requirement to travel and material movement from the River and Sea.

SHIPMENT is the requirement to travel and material movement from River and Sea.

AIRPLANE, HELICOPTER is the further and advanced requirement to travel and material movement from one place to other place in air and space.

FUTURE AIR CAR-Future air car is the further development of Transport which run and fly both.

FUTURE SHIPAIR CAR-Future ship air car is the further development of Transport which can run, swim and fly.

SPACECRAFT is the mode of transport which should have the facility of air, water, food and Environment.

MAGNETO FIELD CRAFT will become the advanced way to move from one place to another place even from EARTH to MOON or other planets in a few minutes as magnet poles attract very fast and diffract very fast.

TRANSPORTATION-

Transportation is the movement of humans, animals, and goods from one location to another. In other words, the action of transport is defined as a particular movement of an organism or thing from a point A (a place in space) to a point B.

Modes of Transport include Walk, Bicycle, MotorCycle, Car, Bus (Land) , water, air, cable, pipeline and Space.

The field can be divided into infrastructure, vehicles and Operations.

Transport enables trade between people, which is essential for the development of Civilization.

Transport infrastructure consists of the fixed installations, including roads, railways, airways, waterways, canals and pipelines and terminals such as airport, railway stations, Bus Stations, waterhouses, trucking terminals, refueling depots (including fueling docks and fuel stations), and seaports.

Terminals may be used both for interchange of passengers and cargo and for maintenance.

Means of transport are any of the different kinds of transport facilities used to carry people or cargo.

They may include vehicles, riding animals, pack animals.

Vehicles may include wagons, automobiles, bicycles, buses, trains, trucks, helicopters, watercrafts, spacecrafts and aircraft.

1—Dirigible Balloon. 2—Aeroplane. 3—Eskimo Dog Team. 4—Prairie Schooner. 5—Russian Troika
6—Reindeer Sledge. 7—Camel: Ship of the Desert. 8—First Railway Train in England, 1825.
9—Modern Railway Train. 10—Automobile.

ECOLOGICAL SUSTAINABILITY-

Sustainability is a societal goal that broadly aims for humans to safely co-exist on planet Earth over a long time.

Specific definitions of sustainability are difficult to agree on and therefore vary in the literature and over time.

Sustainability is commonly described along the lines of three dimensions (also called pillars): environmental, economic and social.

This concept can be used to guide decisions at the global, national and at the individual level (e.g. Sustainable Living).

In everyday usage of the term, sustainability is often focused mainly on the environmental aspects.

The most dominant environmental issues since around 2022 have been climatic change, loss of biodiversity, loss of ecosystem services, land degradation and air and water.[1]

Humanity is now exceeding several "planetary boundaries". Reducing these negative impacts on the environment would improve environmental sustainability

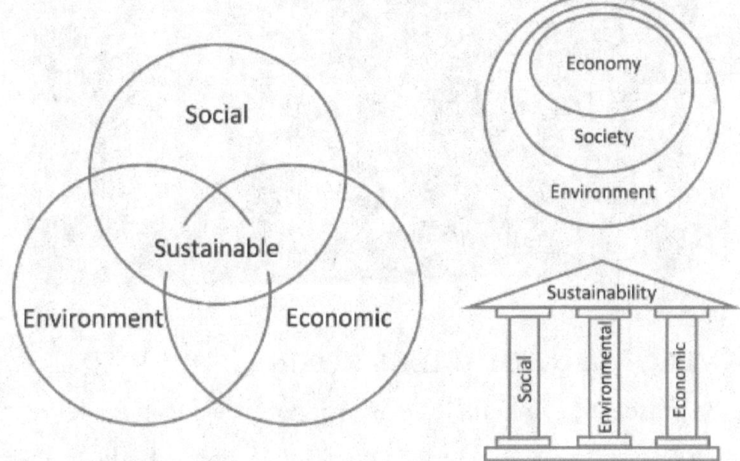

ECOSYSTEM-

An ecosystem (or ecological system) consists of all the organisms and the physical environment with which they interact.

These biotic and abiotic components are linked together through nutrient cycles and energy flows.

Energy enters the system through photosynthesis and is incorporated into plant tissue.

By feeding on plants and on one another, animals play an important role in the movement of matter and energy through the system.

They also influence the quantity of plant and microbial biomass present.

By breaking down dead organic matter, decomposers release carbon back to the atmosphere and facilitate nutrient cycling by converting nutrients stored in dead biomass back to a form that can be readily used by plants and microbes.

DEVELOPMENT OF GREEN ROAD-

In the present day in India Road & Bridge is designed for 15 years only.

When traffic increases after 15 years either the road fails or the road is in congestion or needs something else.

Bridges fail due to congestion, heavy traffic etc.

In today Bridge is normally design to sustain for 100 years, but road is planned for 15 years only accordingly bridge should planned.

In fifteen years both sides of the road town are developing.

Land cost is growing and widening becoming a costly affair and roads becoming a street road.

Requirement and Development of Transportation creates the requirement of Construction of Road not for 15 years or 50 years but for the design of 1000-100000 years such that developed and developing mode of transport should be sustained.

DESIGN OF GREEN ROAD-

GREEN ROAD is a Road which is designed such that quality of Air, Water, Food and Environment should not disturb and possibility of every development of Transport should adjust on the Road forever.

Population Growth-Taken Extreme

Traffic Condition-Extreme

Traffic Congestion-Extreme

Year of Year- Till end of Earth.

Standard Crust Provision-

Subgrade of 500mm which contains Soil/Gravel(50%)+Local Sand/Ganga Sand(25%)+Brick Bats/Gravel/Aggregate(25%)

Base-500mm with Soil(20%)+Brick Bats/Gravel/Aggregate(60%)+Sand(20%)

Wearing Course-Ist Layer thickness-150mm with Cement/Lime(10%)+BrickBats/Gravel/Aggregate(60%)+Silt (10%)+Clay(10%)+Cow dung(10%)

Layer-II(50mm) Bituminous Concrete(5% Bitumen) or 50mm-Cement Concrete(1:2:4)

Path side Drainage- 2m both side-2m, thickness-150mm with similar material of wearing course.

Plantation three Row -15m both side-6m with Neem tree, Peepal tree.

Footpath constructed by Silt-6m each side-10m thickness-300mm with Ganga silt preferably or by prepared at site in same proportion in Ganga silt.

Major Drainage with utility drainage both side2.0mx2.0m+2mx1m-6m

Cross Drainage of Box Culvert of (10mx5.5m)with Duct Drain (5mx5m) @ 250m interval

Similar material used for Pathway wearing Course Layer-I,

Construction.

Solar light should be planned on both sides of the road.

Provision of water supply is also essential.

Provision of Crossing of Utility is also essential at each 500m and Cross drainage of 2mx2m is essential to construct at each 500m.

Public Underpass is essential to construct at every 5km interval for free movement of water, human and utility.Standard size of Underpass should be 55mx7m/100x7/122x7 with thickness of 0.5m

Cross drainage itself can be used for crossing of Utility.

What is Cow Dung?

Cow Dung is the product of COW, OX and Buffalo.Properties of COW DUNG ASH is reduced cement %.

CDA has good binding properties and it reduces voids in concrete.

Physical properties of cow dung:

a) It is bulky

b) It has large ash content

c) It has low volatile content after burning.

d) Carbon content is low

e) Burning ratio is low

f) Low thermal conductivity

g) Eco-friendly material

h) Economical

i) Easily available The constituents of CDA are similar to OPC.

In Portland Cement has main oxides of CaO, Al2O3, and Fe2O3 are more than in CDA.

The combined alkali (Na2O+K2O) is 3.5% in CDA, which is less.

It reduces the chances of disintegration of concrete by AAR.

The SO3 of 1.36% present is below the 4% maximum specified by ASTM C 618-12, hence CDA used in mortar and concrete can improve durability and prevent unsoundness.

What is Soil?

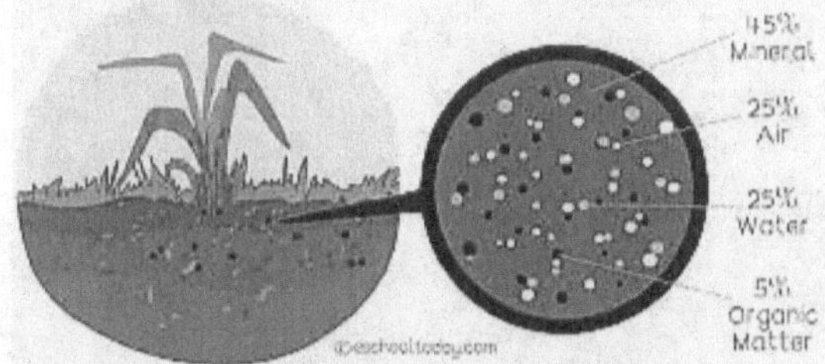

Soil is the mixture of Clay, Silt, Sand, Gravel, stone etc.It also mix with organic and Inorganic material.

sand, loamy sand, sandy loam, loam, silt loam, silt, sandy clay loam, clay loam, silty clay loam, sandy clay, silty clay, and clay.

Soil textures are classified by the fractions of sand, silt, and clay in a soil.

Soils Description Chart

SOIL TYPE		PARTICLE SIZE (mm)	COMPACTNESS / STRENGTH		
Very coarse soil	BOULDERS	200	**Term**	**Field identification of compactness for very coarse soils**	
	COBBLES	60	Loose / Dense	By inspection of voids and particle packing.	Description generally in accordance with BS 5930, 1999. For further information see British Standard.

			Term	**Field identification of compliance for coarse soils**	**Density / SPT 'N' Value Correlation**

SOIL TYPE		PARTICLE SIZE (mm)	Term	Field identification for coarse soils	Density	'N' Value	Ø
Coarse soils	GRAVELS	Coarse 20 / Medium 6 / Fine 2	Loose / Dense	Excavated by spade, 50mm peg driven easily / Requires pick for excavation, 50mm peg hard to drive.	Very Loose	<4	<28°
					Loose	4-10	28-30°
					Medium dense	10-30	30-36°
	SANDS	Coarse 0.6 / Medium 0.2 / Fine 0.06	Slightly cemented	Visual examination; pick removes soil in lumps which can be abraded.	Dense	30-50	36-41°
					Very Dense	>50	>41°

Secondary constituent of coarse soils

Prefix	Suffix	Proportion (%) COARSE	Proportion (%) FINE
Slightly (Sandy)	With a little / Occasional	<5	<5
(Sandy)	With some	5-20	5-15
Very (Sandy)	Much / many	20-40	15-35

SOIL TYPE		PARTICLE SIZE (mm)	Term	Field identification of compactness / strength for Silts	
Fine soils	SILTS	Coarse 0.02 / Medium 0.006 / Fine 0.0002	Soft or Loose	Easily moulded or crushed in the fingers.	
			Firm or Dense	Can be moulded or crushed by strong pressure in the fingers.	

Secondary constituent of fine soils

Prefix	Suffix	Proportion (%)
Slightly (Sandy)	With a little / Occasional	<35
(Sandy)	With some	35-65
Very (Sandy)	Much / many	>65

	Term	**Field identification of Strength for Clays**	Strength
CLAYS	Very Soft	Exudes between fingers when squeezed	<20 kN/m²
	Soft	Moulded by light finger pressure	20-40 kN/m²
	Firm	Moulded by strong finger pressure	40-75 kN/m²
	Stiff	Cannot be moulded - indented by thumb	75-150 kN/m²
	Very Stiff	Indented by thumbnail (hard >300 kN/m²)	>150 kN/m²

SOIL TYPE	PARTICLE SIZE	Term	**Field identification of Consistency for Peats**	Structure
Organic soils ORGANIC CLAY SILT SAND	Varies	Firm	Fibres already compressed together	Fibrous;
PEATS	Varies	Spongy	Very compressible and open structure.	Plant remains recognisable and retain some strength
		Plastic	Can be moulded in hand and smears on fingers	Amorphous. Recognisable plant remains absent.

VISUAL IDENTIFICATION OF SOIL TYPES

BOULDERS	Only seen complete in pits or exposures.
COBBLES	Often difficult to recover from boreholes.
GRAVELS	Easily visible to naked eye, particle shape can be described, grading can be described.
SANDS	Visible to naked eye; very little or no cohesion when dry, grading can be described.
SILTS	Only coarse silt barely visible to naked eye; exhibits little plasticity, slightly granular or silky to the touch. Disintegrates in water, lumps dry quickly, possess cohesion but can be powdered easily between fingers.
CLAYS	Dry lumps can be broken but not powdered between fingers; they also disintegrate under water but more slowly than silt; smooth to the touch, exhibits plasticity; sticks to the fingers and dries slowly; shrinks appreciably on drying usually showing cracks.
ORGANIC SOILS	Contains substantial amounts or organic vegetable matter
PEATS	Predominantly plant remains usually dark brown in colour, often with distinctive smell, low bulk density

freephone: 0800 000 345
www.groundforce.uk.com

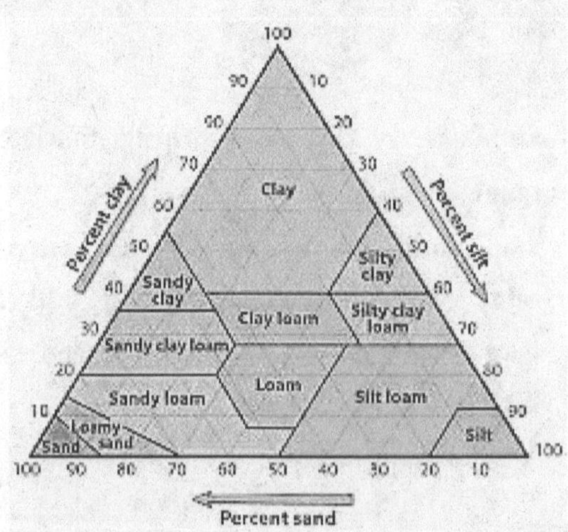

COARSE-GRAINED SOILS		
(more than 50% of material is larger than No. 200 sieve size.)		

GRAVELS More than 50% of coarse fraction larger than No. 4 sieve size			Clean Gravels (Less than 5% fines)
		GW	Well-graded gravels, gravel-sand mixtures, little or no fines
		GP	Poorly-graded gravels, gravel-sand mixtures, little or no fines
			Gravels with fines (More than 12% fines)
		GM	Silty gravels, gravel-sand-silt mixtures
		GC	Clayey gravels, gravel-sand-clay mixtures
SANDS 50% or more of coarse fraction smaller than No. 4 sieve size			Clean Sands (Less than 5% fines)
		SW	Well-graded sands, gravelly sands, little or no fines
		SP	Poorly graded sands, gravelly sands, little or no fines
			Sands with fines (More than 12% fines)
		SM	Silty sands, sand-silt mixtures
		SC	Clayey sands, sand-clay mixtures

What is Silt?

Silt is a granular material of a size between sand and clay and composed mostly of broken grains of quartz.

Size of Silt -(0.002 to 0.06mm)

What is Clay?

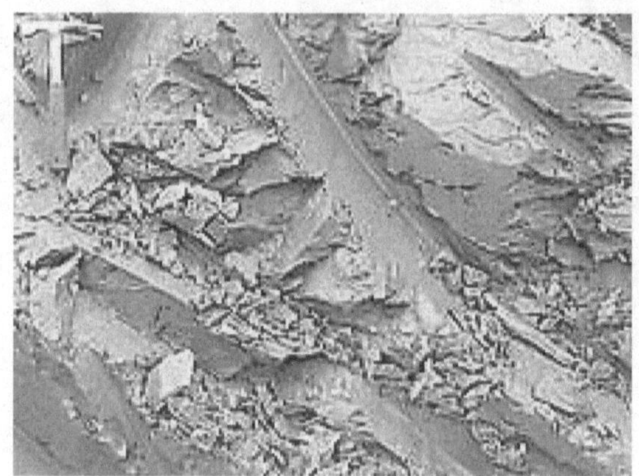

Clay is a type of fine-grained natural soil material containing clay minerals. Clays develop plasticity when wet, due to a molecular film of water surrounding the clay particles, but become hard, brittle and non-plastic upon drying or firing.

'Fine soils' having **at least 35 per cent finer than 0.06mm particle size** and includes silts (0.002 to 0.06mm) and clays below the 0.06mm

What is Gravel?

Gravel is a loose aggregation of rock fragments. Gravel occurs naturally throughout the world as a result of sedimentary and erosive geologic processes; it is also produced in large quantities commercially as crushed stone.

Fragments in gravel range in size from **pebbles (4–64 mm [0.16–2.52 inches] in diameter), through cobbles (64–256 mm [2.52–10.08 inches]), to boulders (larger than 256 mm).**

Gravel, **aggregate of more or less rounded rock fragments coarser than sand** (i.e., more than 2 mm [0.08 inch] in diameter). Gravel beds in some places contain accumulations of heavy metallic ore minerals, such as cassiterite (a major source of tin), or native metals, such as gold, in nuggets or flakes.

What is Jhama Brick Bat?

Brick bats are defined as a cut portion of brick , generally the brick is cutted along the width and the length of the brick piece is smaller than the original.

What is Aggregate?

Construction aggregate, or simply aggregate, is a broad category of coarse- to medium-grained particulate material used in construction, including sand, gravel, crushed stone, slag, recycled concrete and geosynthetic aggregates.

Aggregates are **coarse particulate rock-like material consisting** of a collection of particles ranging in size from < 0.1 mm to > 50 mm.

What is Sand?

Sand is a mixture of small, fine grains of various minerals, materials or rocks.

Sand ranges from **0.05 to 2.0 mm**. Particles larger than 2.0 mm are called gravel or stones.

What is Subgrade?

Subgrade is the native material underneath a constructed road, pavement or railway track.

Subgrade is a material which supports Base and Wearing Coat.

The quality of Subgrade material is such that which sustain the ultimate load.

The standard quality of Subgrade to be as under-

Subgrade of 500mm which contains Soil/Gravel(50%)+Local Sand/Ganga Sand(25%)+Brick Bats/Gravel/Aggregate(25%)

What is Base?

The base layer forms the foundation for the road surface

The bottom layer essentially comprises an unbound mixture of coarse and fine crushed stone, as well as crushed sand, to achieve the desired load-bearing capacity and absorb traffic loads so that the underlying subgrade is not deformed.

It contributes to drainage.

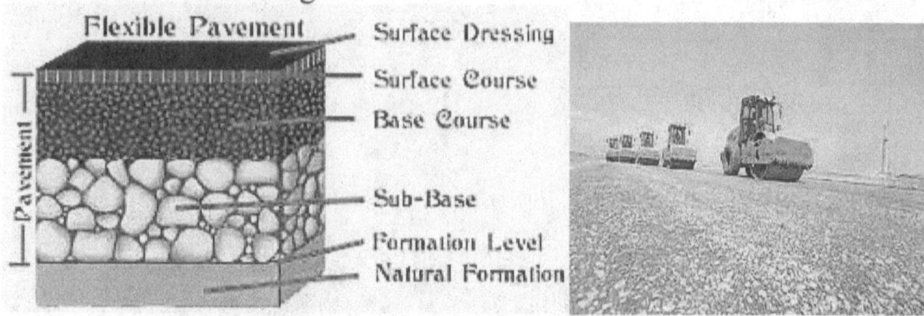

The base course or base course in pavements is a layer of material in an asphalt roadway, race track, riding arena, or sporting field.

Standard Base thickness should be 500mm with Silty Soil(20%)+Brick Bats/Gravel/Aggregate(60%)+Ganga Sand/Sand(20%)

What is wearing Coat?

The wearing course is the upper layer in roadway, airfield, and dockyard construction. The term 'surface course' is sometimes used, however this term is slightly different as it can be used to describe very thin surface layers such as chip seals.

Standard Wearing Course-Ist Layer thickness is150mm with Cement/Lime(5-10%)+BrickBats/Gravel/Aggregate(60%)+Silt(10%) +Clay(10%)+Cow dung(5-10%)+Rice Husk-5%

And standard Wearing Coat Layer-II is (50mm) Bituminous Concrete (5% Bitumen) or 50mm-Cement Concrete(with 10-15% cement)

What is Bituminous Concrete?

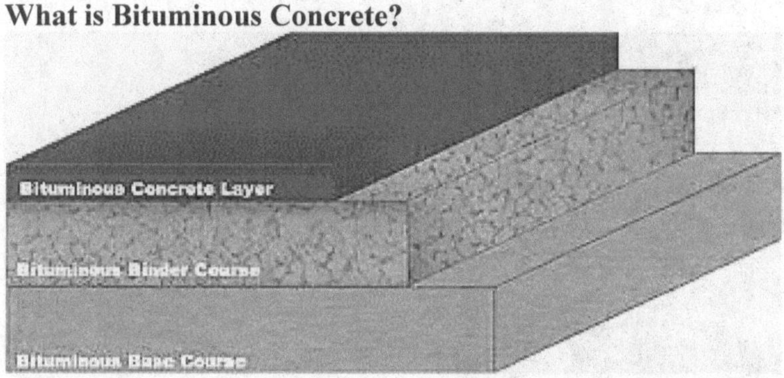

BITUMINOUS CONCRETE means a mixture of petroleum by-products and gravel used for paving to form a smooth, permanent surface. Bituminous Concrete with 5% Bitumen is standardized to implement.

What is cement Concrete.

Concrete is a composite material composed of fine and coarse aggregate bonded together with a fluid cement that hardens over time. Concrete is the second-most-used substance in the world after water, and is the most widely used building material.

Cement comprises from **10 to 15 percent** of the concrete mix, by volume or 12-20% by weight.

What is Earthwork?

Earthworks are engineering works created through the processing of parts of the earth's surface involving quantities of soil or unformed rock.

What is Path side Drainage?

Path Side Drainage are generally constructed parallel to the side of the road and it disposes the surface water efficiently

What is ROW Plantation?

Row Plantation is in a straight line @ 3m in 3m distance from another row.Mainly trees which provide 24x7 oxygen are essential to plants that is Neem, Peepal, Bel, Ashok.

What is a Footpath?

A footpath is a type of thoroughfare that is intended for use only by pedestrians and not other forms of traffic such as motorized vehicles, bicycles and horses.

They can be found in a wide variety of places, from the center of cities, to farmland, to mountain ridges.

This can be prepared with Paver Block or by waste material.

What is a Green Footpath?

A footpath is a type of thoroughfare that is intended for use only by Barefoot pedestrians and not other forms of traffic such as motorized vehicles, bicycles and horses.

They can be found in a wide variety of places, from the center of cities, to farmland, to mountain ridges.

This is Prepared with Silt, Ganga Silt or Soil.

What is Drainage?

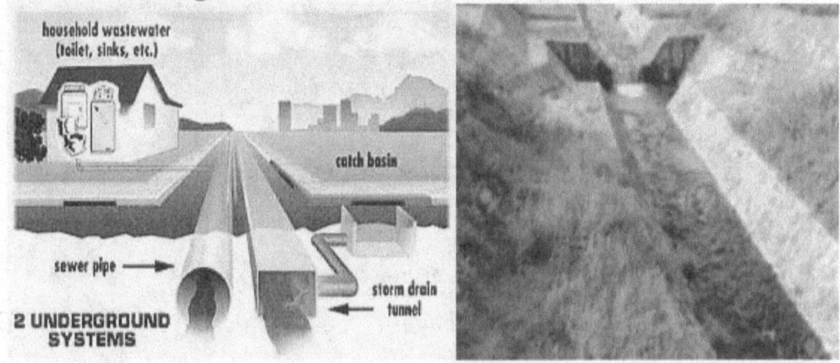

Drainage is the system or process by which water or other liquids are drained from a place.

Preferably and standard drainage design of Box 2.0mx2.0m considered with thickness of 0.2m.98

Line the pots with pebbles to ensure good drainage.

The Kachha drainage system has collapsed because of too much rain, hence drainage has to be restored before and after rain.

What is Cross Drainage and Public Underpass?

Cross Drainage is the system or process by which flow of water, flow of utility, movement of humans should be ensured.

Standard size of Cross drainage is considered is 2mx2m of 0.3m thickness of 0.3m and PUP public Underpass is considered of 55mx7m/100mx7m/122mx7m of 0.5m thickness with Green Concrete.

What is Utility Drainage?

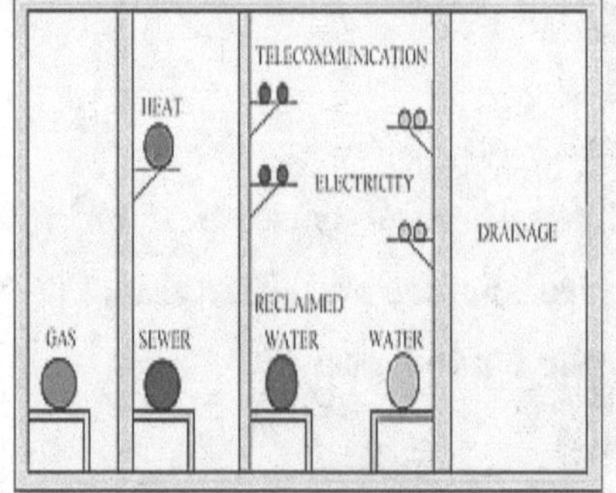

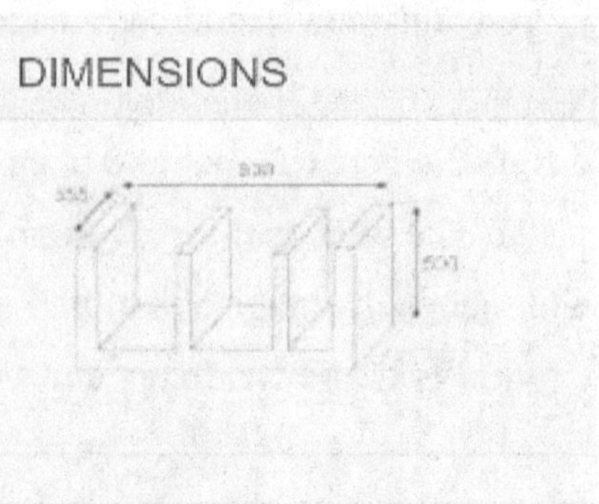

Utility Drainage is the system or process by which a utility such as an electric line, phone line and other line should drain from a place.

Preferably and standard drainage design of Box 2.0mx1.0m considered with thickness of 0.2m.

What is Solar Energy?

Solar power is the conversion of energy from sunlight into electricity, either directly using photovoltaics (PV), indirectly using concentrated solar power, or a combination. Photovoltaic cells convert light into an electric current using the photovoltaic effect.

Solar energy is **a renewable, inexhaustible and affordable form of energy**. It can be used to cook food, heat water, and generate electricity. Furthermore, electrical energy generated from solar energy can be stored in solar cells.

What is Cement?

Cement is a fine gray powder that is mixed with water and other substances to make mortar or concrete. It is a key building material in both residential and commercial construction work.

Concrete is a mixture of cement, gravel, sand, water and a range of aggregates. With about <u>10 billion tons</u> of concrete produced every year, it is the most consumed substance in the world, second only to water.It is also the world's most widely used material for construction – from bridges to large buildings, concrete forms the very foundation of our infrastructure. Over <u>70%</u> of the world's population lives in a concrete structure.

The chief chemical constituents of Portland cement are as follows:

Sr.No.	Description or Components	% Percentage
1	Lime(Cao)	60 to 67%
2	Silica(Sio2)	17 to 25%
3	Alumina(Al2o3)	3 to 8%
4	Iron Oxide(Fe2O3)	0.5 to 6%
5	Magnesia(Mgo)	0.1 to 4%
6	Sulphur Trioxide(So3)	1 to 3%
7	Soda and/or Potash (Na2O+K2O)	0.5 to 1.3%

What are the dangers of cement?

Plasterers, bricklayers and concreters are most at risk. And working with cement can lead to this sensitivity, this allergy, which then later leads to the dermatitis. Your skin can actually get burned by wet cement. These burns can take months to heal, and can even lead to skin grafts, or amputation in extreme case

What is the alternative to cement in future?

The benefits of large scale applications would be countless. There are various other natural materials being tested, experimented with and researched to substitute concrete. **Bamboo, Rammed Earth, Timbercrete, Clay, Strawbale, Grasscrete, Cork and Wool** are some amongst the large pool of innovations.

GREEN CONCRETE-

Green Concrete is the Concrete which does not have sensitivity or allergy which leads dermatitis to the human.

Green Concrete is the Concrete which has a positive impact on the human body and the worker who is touching the cement does not get any harm to the human body.

Green Concrete is a term given to a concrete that has had extra steps taken in the mix design and placement to insure a sustainable structure and a long life cycle with a low maintenance   surface. e.g. Energy saving, CO_2 emissions, waste water.

The combination of Green Concrete is as under-

Cement-5 to 10%+Aggregate-90%+Rice Husk-5-10%

WIDTH OF GREEN ROAD

Traffic in village is minimum, traffic in town is more than the village while traffic in City is more than the Town.Hence to meet the all requirements there are three qualities of Green road has to develop while Town and City have Street Road as specification.In new specification this must be minimum of Village Road.

Road divided in four categories as requirement is as under-
1. STREET ROAD
2. VILLAGE ROAD
3. HIGHWAY
4. EXPRESSWAY/NATIONAL HIGHWAY

PRESENT CONDITION OF ROAD AND THEIR LIMITATION-

1. STREET -

Street is a branch of village road which connects the Village Road.

What is Street?

A Pathway which connects to the Village Road.

Population establishing surrounding streets.

Street should be constructed such that at any time two should move one time.

Humans should walk barefoot, hence footpaths should be prepared by silt not by clay or by aggregate or by gravel.

Both sides of the road, two lanes of trees are essential to cool the Street.

Open side drain is essential to drain off the street water efficiently and Drain should be planned of 2.0mx2.0m with 1mx0.5m utility Drain.

Solar light should be planned on both sides of the road.

Provision of water supply is also essential.

Provision of Crossing of Utility is also essential at each 250m and Cross drainage of 10mx5.5m with duct Drain(5mx5m) is essential to construct at each 250m.

WIDTH OF STREET-

Pathway for vehicle-10m

Path side Drainage- 1m both side-2m

Plantation two Row -3m both side-6m

Footpath constructed by Silt-5m each side-10m

Major Drainage with utility drainage both side 1.5mx1.5m+1mx0.5m-4m<10

Width of Street-10+2+10+10+20=52m

CRUST-

Pathway for vehicle-10m

Subgrade-500mm with Soil(50%)+Sand(25%)+Gravel/Brick bats(25%)

Base-500mm with Soil(20%)+Brick Bats/Gravel/Aggregate(60%)+Sand(20%)

Wearing Course-Ist Layer thickness-150mm with Cement/Lime(5-10%)+Brick Bats/Gravel/Aggregate(60%)+Silt(10%)+Clay(10%)+Cow dung(10%)+Husk(5%)

Path side Drainage- 1m both side-2m, thickness-150mm with similar material of wearing course.

Plantation two Row -3m both side-6m with Neem, Peepal tree.

Footpath constructed by Silt-5m each side-10m thickness-300mm with Ganga silt preferably or by prepared at site in same proportion in Ganga silt.

Major Drainage with utility drainage both side 2.0mx2.0m+1mx0.5m-5m

Similar material used for Pathway Construction.

CROSS SECTION STREET-

STREET-VILLAGE JUNCTION

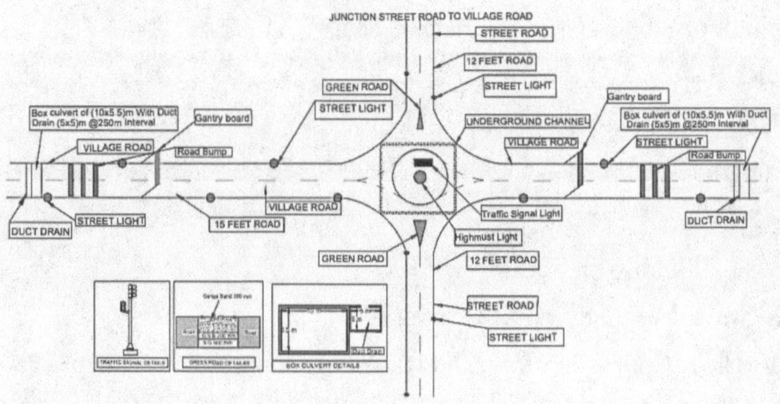

2. VILLAGE ROAD

Village Road which connects village to village and village to HIGHWAY or EXPRESSWAY.

What is a Village?

A village is a clustered human settlement or community, larger than a hamlet, with a population typically ranging from a few hundred to a few thousand to irrigate the land, grow the plantation, Grow the crops like paddy, wheat, bajra, makka, onion, potato, garam Masala, keeping animal to grow and get milk, cow dung, cow urine, growing the organic vegetable, fruits, creating ponds to grow the fishiaries.

Bullock carts and Horse carts are organic vehicles.

Preparing Solar Panels to create light.

Preparing Water Electricity in the flowing channel.

Developing Ayurvedic medicine for their health.

Establishing village Gurukull and teaching Moral value, learning economics and arithmetics, respecting others or elders to create moral value.

Performing natural yoga, such as Barefoot walking, taking a dip in river, ponds or flowing body, taking organic Breakfast, Lunch and Dinner.

Developing Temple, Marriage Hall and Market place to devote, Social requirement and Economics requirement.

Demerits due to Entry of Tractors-

Innovation of the tractor destroyed the whole Economy in village, Now Bullock cart and Horse Cart shifted to Tractor, Motorcycle.People started to plow with Tractor means those person who was involved in this business they are forced to shift the place or died like Charbaha, Dhanuk, halwaha, Katauni left the village and disappeared and serious loss including Ox reaching to slaughter place.Whole Society is disturbed created a instability in society.

A LITTLE CHANGING JUST DEVELOPMENT OF TRACTOR DESTROYED THE WHOLE VILLAGE ECONOMY.

In present condition this road is designed with just 3.75m width carriageway and a total of 7.5m width.1, 875m width both side considered for Hard Shoulder and this area is prepared by treated soil mix with sand, brick bats and aggregate or my moorum or by Gravel.This is suitable in Rainy Season and other season for movement of people, cycle, Motor Bikes, car, Truck, Buses etc.

This is designed for connecting the road with Village, with consideration of traffic or population for 15 years only.

DRAWBACKS-

In future after construction of the Road, various developments will take place, such as people constructing houses nearby the Road, performing their own business etc.

This is not designed such that People should open the outlets of Petrol Pumps, Vehicle Maintenance Store, Police Depot, Health Centre, Shoping Zone, Bus Stoppage, Recreation area.

THIS ROAD IS NOT SUITABLE FOR BAREFOOT WALKING, Which is first and most important for Human Development and HEALTH.

MISSING EARTHEN FOOTPATH means missing Human, Cow, Ox, Buffalo, Horse, Goat, Ass health.

SUSTAINABLE DESIGN-

Village Road is the most important and life line road which connects to village to village and connecting to Highway, Expressway, Railway Station, Airport, Shipyard, Temple, Hospital, School, College, Playground, Marriage Hall, Market Area, Park, Community Hall, Cinema Theater, Cremation Center, Police Station, Municipality, River, Sea, Hill, Forest, Agriculture Land, COW OX shade GAUSHALA etc.

Design of Village Road is challenging, such that it should meet the requirement of year to year.

Design Criteria-

Extreme Population Growth is considered for 10000-100000 years.

Extreme and advanced thinking on Traffic situation and condition.

Extreme and advanced thinking on Human Health.

Design-

Imagine a whole village beside the Road, Village has three crops from agricultural land to provide 24x7 water and Solar energy panel for 24x7 light, Village has technology to utilize the OX, COW in agriculture Economy.

Villages have GURUKUL, Health Center, Business Center, Temple, Community hall, Marriage Hall, Playground, Police Station, Village Municipal.

Cinema Hall, Cremation Place.Village has different small scale industries.

Each family has a Bullock Cart/Car, Horse Cart/MotorCycle, Cycle to travel from one place to other place and Barefoot walking for Agriculture work and Local movement.

Roads are designed such that Vehicle movement, movement of pure air, Environment should not be disturbed.

Normally Village people have the mentality to park the vehicle on Road itself, hence One lane on both sides of road is essential to park the vehicle.

Two lanes are required to free in between to allow movement of the vehicle.hence minimum four lane is the essential requirement.

Greenery has equal importance than roads to reduce the developed sound pollution, disturbed CO_2, SO_2, NO_2, dust particles in air.as Road is for vehicles.

Green Belt is for walking for Barefoot, Laying of drainage, Power, water supply from one point to other point to utilize the technology of OX, Industry based on OX such as milling of Oil, Juice etc.Providing solar panel for power 24x7, In water channel electricity should be produced by OX technology.

Provision of Crossing of Utility is also essential at each 500m and Cross drainage of 2mx2m is essential to construct at each 500m.Cross drainage itself can be used for crossing of Utility.

Provision of Public UnderPass of (55mx7m) is essential to construct at each 5km, to have free movement of population.

Provision of Crossing of Utility is also essential at each 250m and Cross drainage of 10mx5.5m with duct Drain(5mx5m) is essential to construct at each 250m.

Provision of Steel Footover Bridge is required at Bus Stoppage to cross from one end to other.

A standard design of Village Road is prepared on the basis of Past development, Present development and Future development is below.

A village road at every 10 km Corridor of 500m(Extra 5m for parking and Greenbelt should increased from 10m to 21m) should be developed to have a Green Petrol Pump/Charging unit, Vehicle Rescue Point, Bus stoppage, Recreation area, Health Center, Police station, Local Market area, Food stall and Rest area to fulfill the needs of Yatri.

Standard crust is described above to follow for each Road.

Standard Road Section is described below-

WIDTH OF VILLAGE ROAD-

Pathway for vehicle-13m

Path side Drainage- 1m both side-2m

Plantation three Row -10m both side-20m

Footpath constructed by Silt-5m each side-10m in Green area.

Major Drainage with utility drainage both side 2mx2m+1mx1m-6m<20m

Width of Street-13+2+20+20=55m

At Corridor-13+2+5+10+21+20=71m

CRUST-

Pathway for vehicle-13m

Subgrade-500mm with Soil(50%)+Sand(25%)+Gravel/Brick bats(25%)

Base-500mm with Soil(20%)+Brick Bats/Gravel/Aggregate(60%)+Sand(20%)

Wearing Course-Ist Layer thickness-150mm with

Cement/Lime(10%)+Brick Bats/Gravel/Aggregate(60%)+Silt(10%)+Clay(10%)+Cow dung(10%)

Wearing Coat-IInd layer with 50mm Bituminous Concrete(5%Bitumen)/Cement Concrete(10%-15% Cement)

Path side Drainage- 1m both side-2m, thickness-150mm with similar material of wearing course.

Plantation three Row -10mx2-20m with Neem, Peepal tree, Ashok(24x7 Oxygen transmitted tree).

Footpath constructed by Silt-5m each side-10m in Green area thickness-300mm with Ganga silt preferably or by prepared at site in same proportion in Ganga silt.

Corridor should developed at every 10km interval with green construction of Police station(25mx16m), Health Centre-(50mx16m), Rescue Area(50mx16m), Refreshment Area(125mx16m), Market Area(125mx16m), Bus Stoppage area(75mx16m), Rest Area(25mx16m), Petrol Pump(25mx16m)

Major Drainage with utility drainage both side 2mx2m+1mx1m-6m<20m

Similar material used for Pathway Construction.

CROSS SECTION OF VILLAGE ROAD

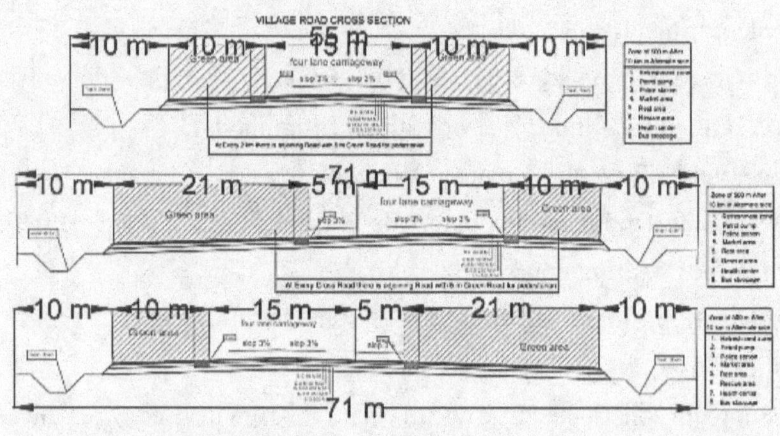

JUNCTION OF VILLAGE ROAD TO VILLAGE ROAD

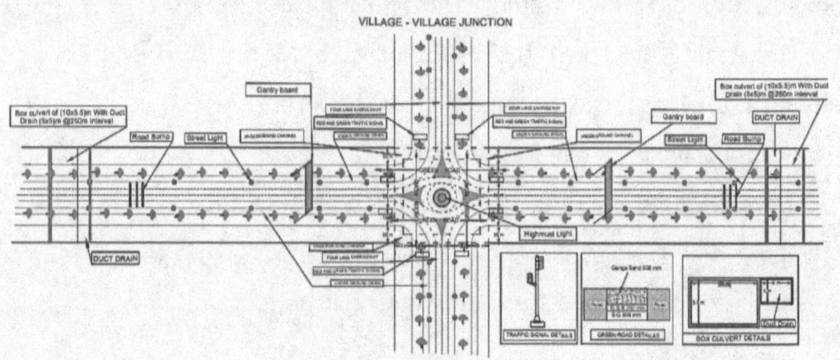

3. HIGHWAY-

Road connecting to two towns and joining to Expressway/National Highway and allowing village roads to join.

What is Town?

Based on the needs of humans, a Village is developed, further based on needs at the junction of few villages, a joint marketplace developing, People from various villages joining each other and arranging some Mela or performing Yagya or Tirth or for other auspicious activity.

In today's definition this is a marketplace where various villagers reach and sell products to each other and sometimes arrange Mela etc to have a family get together.

Previously this was called a HAT, now it is called MARKETPLACE.

Due to the Market various types of businessmen staying and purchasing and selling the product.In one town other towns merchants reach to purchase the product which is available in the same market but not in their market.Hence this area needs more vehicles, Good Road condition etc.

Hence the Road connecting from one Town to Other Town and connecting to Expressway and allowing village roads to join is called HIGHWAY.

PRESENT CONDITION-
State Highway, Other District Road, District Road is the name today.

In present condition this road is designed with various specification and design such as width of carriageway should be 4.5m, 5m, 6m, 7m, 10, 12m, 15m 1.5m width both side considered for Hard Shoulder and this area is prepared by treated soil mix with sand, brick bats and aggregate or moorum or by Gravel.This is suitable in Rainy Season and other season for movement of people, cycle, Motor Bikes, car, Truck, Buses etc.

1m to 5m is generally designed as a Median Green Zone and 5m each side is the Green Zone.

This is designed for connecting the road withTown, with consideration of traffic or population for 15 years only.

SUSTAINABLE DESIGN-

Highway is the most important and lifeline road which connects to Town to Town and connects to Highway, Expressway, and Village Road.

Highway design is challenging, such that it should meet the requirement of year to year.

Design Criteria-

Extreme Population Growth is considered for 10000 yrs to 100000 yrs.

Extreme and advanced thinking on Traffic situation and condition.

Extreme and advanced thinking on Human Health.

Design-

Town is also a village where more people perform business, hence a big market area is required.Once business people moving and staying means Dharamshala is essential, Production of Electricity, Production of various fooding items, sweets, production of clothes, book, paper, shoe, chappal etc.

Town will develop GURUKUL, Health Center, Business Center, Temple, Community hall, Marriage Hall, Playground, Police Station,

Town Municipal.

Cinema Hall, Cremation Place.Town has different small scale industries.

Each family has a Bullock Cart/Car, Horse Cart/MotorCycle, Cycle to travel from one place to other place and Barefoot walking for Agriculture work and Local movement.

Highways are designed such that Vehicle movement, movement of pure air, Environment should not be disturbed.

Two lanes are required to free in between to allow free movement of the vehicle.hence minimum four lane is the essential requirement.

Town to Town Length is more hence, vehicles will take speed and to maintain the speed one way is essential, hence design includes Central Median Green Belt-10m, Lane-15mx2, Green Belt-15mx2, Drainage-10mx2.

Greenery has equal importance than roads to reduce the developed sound pollution, disturbed CO_2, SO_2, NO_2, dust particles in air.as Road is for vehicles.

Green Belt is for walking for Barefoot, Laying of drainage, Power, water supply from one point to other point to utilize the technology of OX in the same technology electricity should be produced, Providing solar panels for power 24x7.

Provision of Crossing of Utility is also essential at each 250m and Cross drainage of 10mx5.5m with Duct Drain (5mx5m)is essential to construct at each 250m.

Provision of Public UnderPass of (100mx7m) is essential to construct at each 5km, to have free movement of population.

Provision of Steel Flyover staircase(5m width) is required at Bus

Stoppage to cross from one end to other.

A standard design of Highway is prepared on the basis of Past development, Present development and Future development as below.

In Highway at every 10km Corridor of 500m with extra parking zone of 5.5m and one side green area increased from 10m to 21m should be developed to have a Green Petrol Pump/Charging unit(25mx16m), Vehicle Rescue Point(50mx16m), Bus stoppage(75mx16m), Recreation area(125mx16m), Health Centre(50mx16m), Police station(25mx16m), Local Market area(125mx16m), Food stall and Rest area(25mx16m) to fulfill the needs of Yatri.

Standard crust is described above to follow for each Road.

Standard Highway Section is described below-

WIDTH OF HIGHWAY-

Pathway for vehicle-14mx2

Path side Drainage- 1mx2 -2m

Plantation three Row in Median -10m

Plantation three Row in Green Area 15mx2-30m

Footpath constructed by Silt-5m each side-10m in Green area.

Major Drainage with utility drainage both side 2mx2m+1mx1m-6m<20m

Width of Highway-14+10+14+2+15+15+20=100m

Width of Highway at Corridor-14+10+10+2+15+5.5+21+20=111.5m

CRUST-

Pathway for vehicle-14mx2

Subgrade-500mm with Soil(50%)+Sand(25%)+Gravel/Brick bats(25%)

Base-500mm with Soil(20%)+Brick

Bats/Gravel/Aggregate(60%)+Sand(20%)

Wearing Course-Ist Layer thickness-150mm with Cement/Lime(10%)+Brick

Bats/Gravel/Aggregate(60%)+Silt(10%)+Clay(10%)+Cow dung(10%)

Wearing Coat-IInd layer with 50mm Bituminous Concrete(5%Bitumen)/Cement Concrete(10%-15% Cement)

Path side Drainage-1mx2-2m, thickness-150mm with similar material of wearing course.

Plantation three Row in Median -10m with Neem, Peepal tree, Ashok(24x7) Oxygen transmitted tree).

Plantation three Row in Green Area-15mx2=30m with Neem, Peepal tree, Ashok(24x7)Oxygen transmitted tree.

Footpath constructed by Silt-5m each side-10m in Green area thickness-300mm with Ganga silt preferably or by prepared at site in same proportion in Ganga silt.

Major Drainage with utility drainage both side 2mx2m+1mx1m-6m<20m

Similar material used for Pathway Construction.

CROSS SECTION OF HIGHWAY

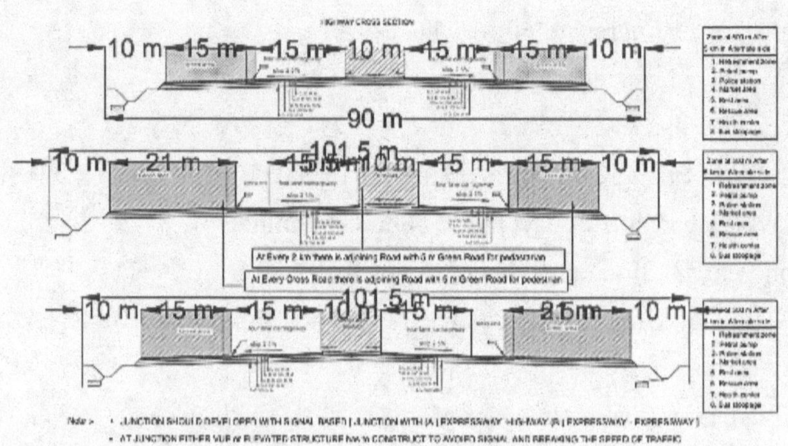

JUNCTION OF HIGHWAY TO HIGHWAY

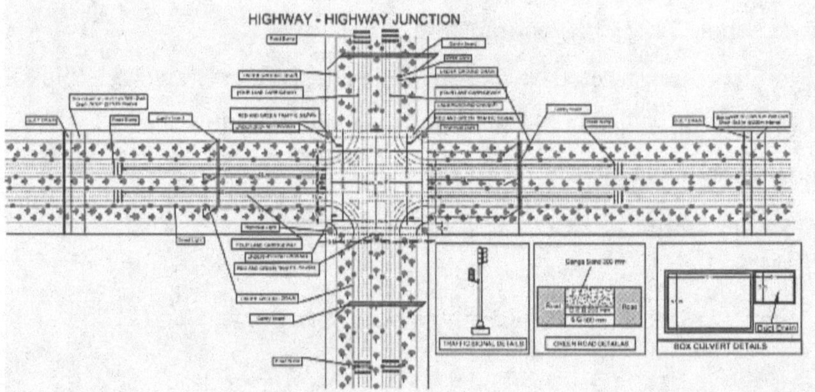

4. EXPRESSWAY/NATIONAL HIGHWAY CONNECTING AIRPORT , METRO RAILWAY, PORT & SPACE (ANTRIKSH) STATION.

Road Connecting to major cities and allowing village roads and highways to join.

What is a City?

CITY is a development for specific activity, specific business, specific

Tirth etc where humans get settlement permanently for specific business, activity or Tirth to ensure the pure air, pure water and pure environment.

Various types of City developing ia as under-

1. City is for Wholesale Marketing.Ex.-Patna City
2. Capital City.Ex-Patna
3. Steel City-Ex.-Jamshedpur
4. Tirth City-Ex.-Jagarnath Puri, Devghar, Gaya, Tirumala, Vatican City, Haridwar
5. Industrial City-Dhanbad for Koylanchal
6. Education City-Dehradun

What is Major city?

A City where a multi city is attached is called a Major City to ensure the pure air, pure water and pure environment.In India not a single city which has the quality of Major City including New Delhi, Kolkata, Mumbai, Chennai etc.

PRESENT CONDITION-

National Highway is the EXPRESSWAY, in present condition.

This EXPRESSWAY is designed with various specification and design such as width of carriageway should be 5m, 7m, 10m, 12m, 15m, 30m and 1.5m width both side considered for Hard Shoulder and this area is prepared by treated soil mix with sand, brick bats and aggregate or moorum or by Gravel.This is suitable in Rainy Season and other season for movement of people, cycle, Motor Bikes, car, Truck, Buses etc.

1m to 5m is generally designed as a Median Green Zone and 5m each side is the Green Zone.

This is designed for connecting the road withTown, with consideration of traffic or population for 15 years only.

SUSTAINABLE DESIGN-

EXPRESSWAY is the most important and lifeline road connecting Airport, Metro Rail, Port and connects City to City and connects to Highway, Expressway, and Village Road.

Expressway design is challenging, such that it should meet the requirement of year to year.

Design Criteria-

Extreme Population Growth is considered for 10000 yrs to 100000 yrs.

Extreme and advanced thinking on Traffic situation and condition.

Extreme and advanced thinking on Human Health.

Design-

City is a Town is also a village where more people perform business or specific activity like Capital City, Textile City, Tirth City, Education City, Port etc hence a big market area is required.Once business people moving and staying means Dharamshala or Hostel or Hotel is essential.

Production of Electricity, Production of various fooding items, sweets, production of clothes, book, paper, shoe, chappal etc.

CITY will develop GURUKUL, Health Center, Business Center, Temple, Community hall, Marriage Hall, Playground, Police Station, Town Municipal.Park etc.

Cinema Hall, Cremation Place.City has different small scale industries.

Each family has a Bullock Cart/Car, Horse Cart/MotorCycle, Cycle to travel from one place to other place and Barefoot walking for Health work and Local movement.

Expressways are designed such that Vehicle movement, movement of pure air, Environment should not be disturbed.

Two lanes are required to free in between to allow free movement of the vehicle.hence minimum six lane is the essential requirement.

City to City Length is more hence, vehicles will take speed and to maintain the speed one way is essential, hence design includes Central Median Green Belt-10m, Main Lane-21mx2, Green Belt-21mx2, Joining Lane-15mx2, Green Zone-10mx2, Metro Rail-5mx2, and Drainage-10mx2.

Greenery has equal importance than Highways to reduce the developed sound pollution, disturbed CO_2, SO_2, NO_2, dust particles in air.as Road is for vehicles.

Green Belt is for walking for Barefoot, Laying of drainage, Power, water supply from one point to other point to utilize the technology of OX in the same technology electricity should be produced, Providing solar panels for power 24x7.

Provision of Crossing of Utility is also essential at each 250m and Cross drainage of 10mx5.5m with Duct Drain(5mx5m) is essential to construct at each 250m.

Provision of Public UnderPass of (122mx7m) is essential to construct at each 5km, to have free movement of population.

Provision of Steel Flyover staircase(5m width) is required at Bus Stoppage to cross from one end to other.

A standard design of Expressway is prepared on the basis of Past development, Present development and Future development as below.

In Expressway at every 5km Corridor of 500m with extra parking zone of 7.5m should be developed to have a Green Petrol Pump/Charging unit(25mx16m), Vehicle Rescue Point(50mx16m), Bus stoppage (75mx16m), Recreation area(125mx16m), Health Center (50mx16m), Police station(25mx16m), Local Market area(125mx16m), Food stall and Rest area(25mx16m) to fulfill the needs of Yatri.

In Expressway at every 50km Corridor of 2000m with extra parking zone of 5m in 15m width Road and Outer Green area width will increase from 10m to 21m should be developed as a Airport station(1km) and Metro Station(1km) to have a Security checking point & Ticket counter as per needs, Green Petrol Pump/Charging unit(25mx16m), Vehicle Rescue Point(50mx16m), Bus stoppage(75mx16m), Recreation area(125mx16m), Health Center (50mx16m), Police station(25mx16m), Local Market area(125mx16m), Food stall and Rest area(25mx16m) to fulfill the needs of Yatri.

Standard crust is described above to follow for each Road.

Standard Highway Section is described below-

WIDTH OF EXPRESSWAY-

Main Pathway for vehicle-20mx2

Path side Drainage- 1mx2 -2m

Joining Lane for vehicle-14mx2

Joining Lane Path side Drainage-1mx2 -2m

Plantation three Row in Median -10m

Plantation Five Row in Green Area 21mx2-42m

Plantation Three Row in Green Area 10mx2=20m

Footpath constructed by Silt-5m each side-10m in Green area.

Major Drainage with utility drainage both side 2mx2m+1mx1m-6m<20m

Width of Expressway-20+2+20+10+14+14+2+10+10+5+5+20=132m

Width of Expressway at Corridor-
20+2+20+7.5+10+14+14+2+10+10+5+5+20=139.5m

Width of Expressway at Airport/Railway-
20+2+20+10+14+14+2+21+21+5+5+20=154m

Width of Expressway at Port for 5km-
20+2+20+10+14+14+2+21+21+15+15+20=174m

Airport Design- International Standard design of Airport is considered.

Size of Airport should be 5.5kmx700m

Width and Length of Runway-80mx5000m

Width of Taxiway 300m should be taken as per Airport Standard.

Drainage to be considered as per Airport standard.

Railway Junction should be developed as per Railway Standard.This contains mainly Broad Gauge, Metre Gauge and Narrow Gauge.

Port should be considered at every 50km stretch of Seashore of Size-(5km x 1km)

Two Lane Goods Train route each side of Incoming and outgoing is considered which will start from inside the port and it will run parallel to Metro Rail and within 5km of length Goods train will connect to Railway regular route.

Port design is considered as per International Standard to ease the movement of public and Goods supply by Road.

Goods train connectivity as a station is the priority.

In Future Space Station will become the special needs of Human Being.People will travel to space and other planet for development and exchange.

Space Station should be considered at every 500 SQUARE KM stretch of Size-(2km x 2km)

One Lane Goods Train route each side of Incoming and outgoing is considered which will start from inside the Space and it will run parallel to Metro Rail and within 5km of length Goods train will connect to Railway regular route.

Space Station design is considered as per International Standard to ease the movement of public and Goods supply by Road.

Goods train connectivity as a station is the priority.

CRUST-

Pathway for vehicle-20mx2

Pathway for Joining Lane-14mx2

Subgrade-500mm with Soil(50%)+Sand(25%)+Gravel/Brick

bats(25%)

Base-500mm with

Soil(20%)+Brick   Bats/Gravel/Aggregate(60%)+Sand(20%)

Wearing Course-Ist Layer thickness-150mm with

Cement/Lime(10%)+Brick

Bats/Gravel/Aggregate(60%)+Silt(10%)+Clay(10%)+Cow dung(10%)

Wearing Coat-IInd layer with 50mm Bituminous

Concrete(5%Bitumen)/Cement Concrete(10%-15% Cement)

Path side Drainage-1mx2-2m, thickness-150mm with similar material of wearing course.

Plantation three Row in Median -10m with Neem, Peepal tree, Ashok(24x7) Oxygen transmitted tree).

Plantation three Row in Green Area-15mx2=30m with Neem, Peepal tree, Ashok(24x7)Oxygen transmitted tree.

Footpath constructed by Silt-5m each side-10m in Green area thickness-300mm with Ganga silt preferably or by prepared at site in same proportion in Ganga silt.

Major Drainage with utility drainage both side 2mx2m+1mx1m-6m<20m

Similar material used for Pathway Construction.

CROSS SECTION OF EXPRESSWAY

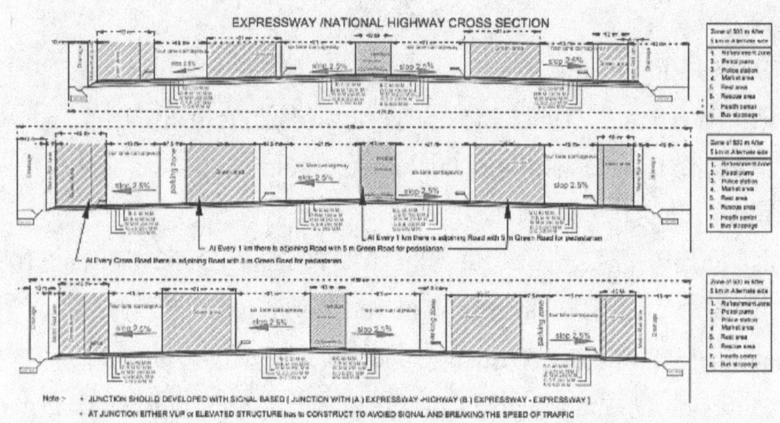

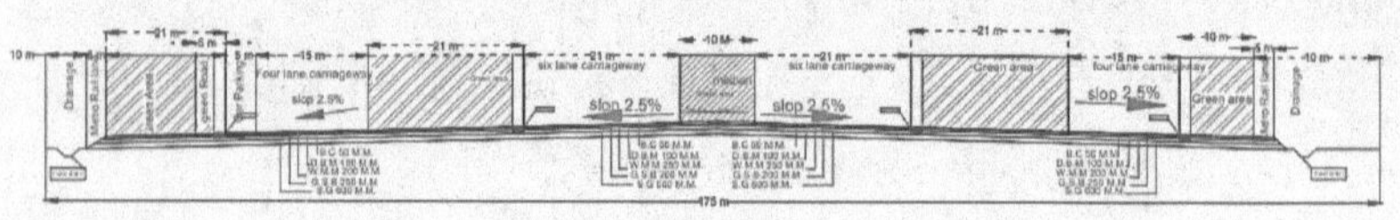

JUNCTION OF EXPRESSWAY TO EXPRESSWAY

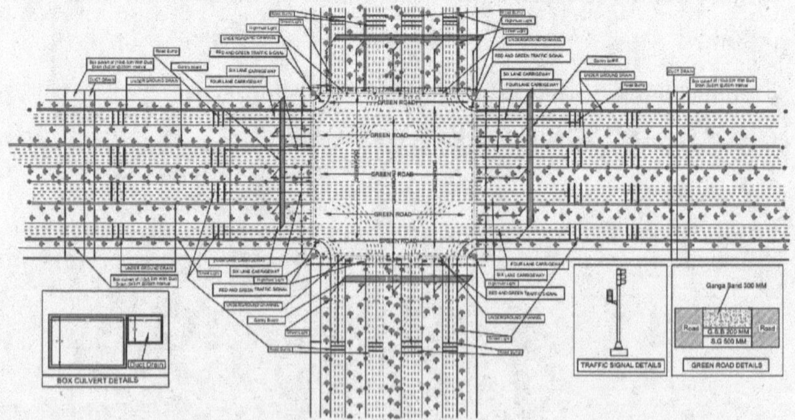

JUNCTION OF EXPRESSWAY-AIRPORT-METRO RAIL

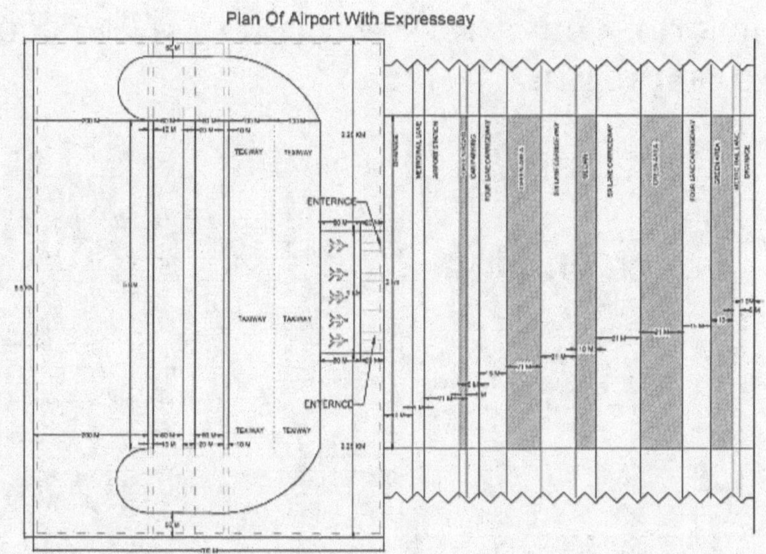

JUNCTION OF EXPRESSWAY-PORT-GOODS RAIL- METRO RAIL

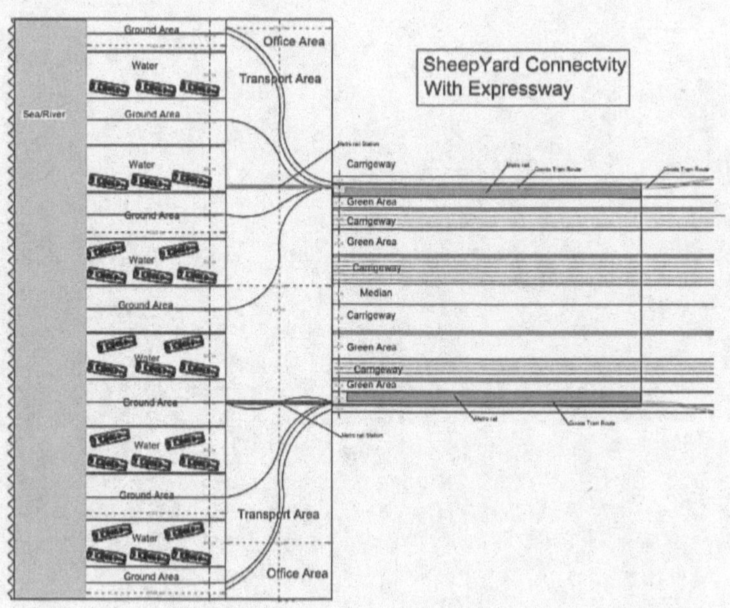

JUNCTION OF EXPRESSWAY-SPACE STATION-GOODS RAIL-METRO RAIL

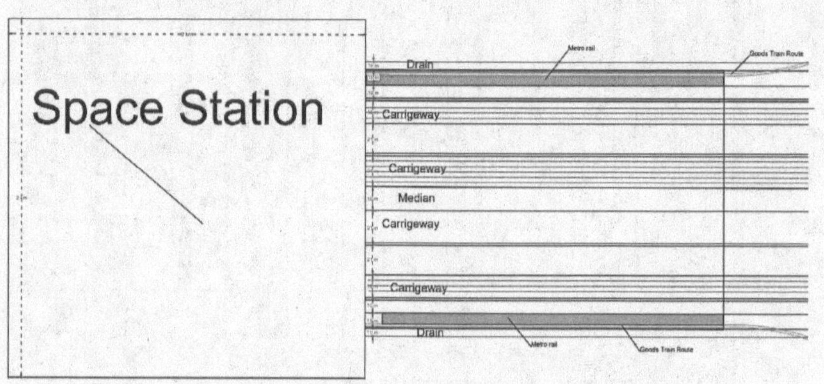

This is essential to understand the economics of Green Road Concept., hence in the next session we will discuss the same.

CHAPTER-14

What is the Economics of Green Road?

Present Economics of Road-

In Today economic concern, the Government is in heavy loss reason is as under-

1. Designing the road for 15 years.means after construction new economics developed in the surrounding area. If the govt will think of purchasing the land, it will be a costly affair.

2. Road became inadequate after a few years of construction.

3. Speed slows down and reconstruction takes more time and is costly.

4. Govt.collecting surcharge as a **TOLL** after collecting the Road tax and tax on Petrol Diesel.

5. Production of Electricity is nil, production from plants is very low.

SUSTAINABLE ECONOMICS INCLUDES-

1. Planning of Road.Planning is the first essential tool to think about the Road.

2. Cost of Land.-Initially when there was no development cost of land is minimum.There is minimum cost involved to purchase the Land.

3. Development Cost.Planning is important to reduce the Development Cost.

4. Maintenance Cost is a regular requirement.

5. Health Cost is the prime cost for human life, hence design includes this cost to save health in all respects.

6. Sustainability Cost is fixed for a long era.One Expenditure is valid

for thousands of years.

7.   Definition of Town and City Road, Example is Capital Road, Steel Road, Tirth Road etc defining the area is specialized, causing other business should not be allowed in the same Town or City. If EXPRESSWAY Joining KOLKATA CAPITAL TO DEVGHAR TIRTH to PATNA CAPITAL TO PRAYGRAJ TIRTH TO KANPUR INDUSTRIAL TO DELHI CAPITAL TO CHANDIGARH CAPITAL TO AMRITSAR INDUSTRIAL TO KASHMIR CAPITAL. A Similar example of Town Road is Lakhisarai Town-Mokama To-Barh To-Bakhtiyarpur To-Patna SahebTown.Similarly village Road is Hasanpur Village-Mahisona Village-Sharma Village.

Capital Road means that place is only a capital not other.Industrial means specific Industry located in that area.

PATNA is the capital of Bihar does not mean Patna should have Wholesale Market or Institution area.This should be separated not mixed.One Place is for one specialization.

Income from the Road-

It includes as under

1.   Road Tax on vehicles is a routine activity.

2.   Toll tax collection on vehicles is the drawback, reducing the speed of vehicles and punishment to the Public.

3.   Road Tax on Petrol, Bio Petrol, and Diesel is also a routine activity.

4.   Production of Electricity by Solar panels is a new activity.

5.   Production of Electricity by Water flow meter is also a new development.

6.   Income from Plantation is huge, as much plantation is now on the Road side.

7. Saving of Land Cost due to increase of Land Cost in future.

8. Decrease of Accidents, Increased width and separation of Road will cause decrease of accidents automatically and speed up the Vehicle.

9. Increase of vehicle speed.A international problem should be resolved.

10. Improvement of health due to Barefoot walk.A fundamental health concern should be improved.

11. Environmental Control due to Tree plantation.AIR, WATER and ENVIRONMENT is the serious concern, plantation will help to control.

12. Right & Systematic Development should take place due to limited specialization to Road.

13. At every 50km Airport Corridor, Metro Corridor is considered to doctail and ease the connectivity of Transportation.

14. At Every 100km of Seashore and in Major river Port Corridor is considered and doctailing with Expressway with Metro & Goods Train Connectivity is the added advantage to doctail the all Transport system.

15. Future development of the Space Station is also designed at every 500km stretch of Seashore and has connection with the Expressway with connectivity of Goods Trains.

16. New development of Air cars, Water cars can run on the road easily.

17. In summer season Drainage area should be utilized to supply the water to Land to have good borewell.

18. Trams are eligible to run on village and Town Road to ease the movement of Public.

19. Underground Metro should develop in Drainage area(5m both sides) to speed up the movement of humans.

20. Crossing of Railway is also essential to speed up the vehicle.

21. Income from the Corridor is a routine profit.

a. Police Station.(25mx16m)

b. Health Centre.(50mx16m)

c. Refreshment Area.(125mx16m)

d. Rescue Area(50mx16m)

e. Market Area(125mx16m)

f. Bus Stoppage area(75mx16m)

g. Rest Area(25mx16m)

h. Petrol Pump/Recharge Center/Gas Center(25mx16m)

CHAPTER-15

What is CONCLUSION of the BOLBAM TIRTH & GREEN ROAD CONCEPT?

Traveling is the requirement of every human being.Travelling in pure air is the requirement of the present in the country.

Traveling by Barefoot is the medicine of human beings, hence Constructing the Road with Green Concept is the requirement of Society.

Bolbam Tirth is the starting of Economy to join the team and reaching to Destination is a result of economy.

BOLBAM TIRTH is a very old method for purification of Human body to just walk for 100km in fasting in a disciplined manner to take the Uttarayani Ganga Jal to put on Shivling.There is a fusion of energy taking place to clean the human body.

Hence BOLBAM TIRTH is the starting of Economy and GREEN ROAD CONCEPT is the development of Bolbam Tirth to enrich the economy from scratch to Extreme and is the excellent tool to purify the Human body and Speedup the vehicle.

16. FURTHER STUDY-

Design and Construction of Bridge is challenging.

A Specific research is required to finding a way to construct the Bridge is of Long Age.

Jai Bihar. Bolbum, Bolbum, Bolbum. Jai Jharkhand.